SURFER'S GUIDE TO HAWAII

HAWAII GETS ALL THE BREAKS!

By Greg Ambrose
Graphics: Kevin Hand
Cover photo: Pipeline, by Warren Bolster

THE BESS PRESS

3565 Harding Ave, Honolulu, Hawai'i 96816
(808) 734-7159 fax (808) 732-3627 www.besspress.com

For Lindsey Carissa and Norene Elena,
two of Kanaloa's finest. Me ke aloha nui loa.

Without the help of some very special people, this book would have lived its entire short life as merely an idea. Mahalo nui loa to: Tim Ryan, for prodding me into action; John Flanagan, for technical expertise; Paul Haraguchi, for giving me a dim glimmering of whither the weather and why I should care; Susan Scott and Craig Thomas for showing me that it could be done; mad genius Kevin Hand for making me laugh just as I was prepared to strangle him; John Ralph Kukeakalani Clark for his advice, encouragement and wisdom; Buddy, Revé, Mike, Sharon, and Maile for being such great people to work with; Warren, Mike and Eric for sharing their visions of the ocean; Norene for keeping me from going off the deep end; every surfer who ever gave me a wave; and especially to the ocean for all the hard-learned lessons and deeply appreciated pleasure.

Author photo: Carlos Viti

Library of Congress Catalog Card No.: 91-70850

Ambrose, Greg
    A Surfer's Guide to Hawaii
Honolulu, Hawaii: Bess Press, Inc.
160 pages

ISBN: 0-935848-90-8

Copyright © 1991 by
The Bess Press, Inc.
Second printing June 1992
Third printing January 1996
Fourth printing January 2000

Hi, I'm
Kuk A. Lloyd.
I'll be escorting
you through the
hazards of Hawaii.
We'll have a
grand time.

TABLE OF CONTENTS

INTRODUCTION

This is not a comprehensive list of all the surf spots in the Hawaiian Islands, but rather an intimate look at some of the finest wave zones in the state. It is intended to help you get off to a good start on your Hawaiian odyssey, but the rest is up to you.

If you're the kind of surfer who embodies the aloha spirit of friendliness and sharing, you'll certainly make friends who will be glad to turn you on to the rest of Hawaii's treasure trove of surf spots.

ALOHA

If the world's supply of aviation fuel evaporated overnight and left airliners stranded on runways like beached whales, there would still be enough surfers in Hawaii to make sure no waves escaped to the beach unridden.

But the jetliners keep arriving every day, disgorging their endless lines of surfers from all corners of the world.

The waves in Hawaii are crowded, and when the waves are really good it's standing room only in the lineup at the more famous surf spots.

No one is going to be particularly thrilled to see you paddling out. And with a local population of red-hot wave slashers and visitors that includes the world's top pros and underground surf heroes, there is nothing you can do on a wave that is going to blow anybody's mind.

Surfers might bang their heads on their boards and howl as you demolish your home break, but in Hawaii you'll just be another anonymous face in the lineup. Unless you do something so astounding, so radical that people will notice you right away: smile.

The vibe level is so intense at times that the lineup seems like the intimidation warm-up at a full-contact karate tournament. You can practice scowling all you want, but you'll never come close to matching the Nanakuli death stare that so many local surfers have perfected.

So relax, loosen up, and smile. Act like you're having fun in the waves, and before you know it, you will be having a grand time. And your mood just might become infectious. Surfers who would otherwise snarl at you might smile back and decide that you're OK.

Talk to people. Everyone has an interesting story to tell, and you'll never hear it if you don't open your mouth first. Compliment someone on a particularly nifty ride, and you might make a friend. Even if your pleasantries don't earn you any waves, they will certainly keep you from getting into a fight.

1

If your fun surf session has been turned into a nightmare by an endless stream of wave-snatching trolls, hang out on the inside section and watch the show. Check out the performances, learn some new techniques and be alert to pounce on the waves that slip past the pack.

It's much less frustrating than trying to battle for waves on the outside peak with the most ferocious surfers in the world.

It used to be possible to sneak away from the crowd to the less famous and less photographed spots, but that idea is shared by too many people now.

With a few clever moves, you can still catch a few waves to yourself. Many surfers are too sluggish to arise for a dawn session, and many surfers are too hungry and burned out to linger through the day's last hour of light.

The noonday sun also seems to evaporate the crowd, and if you can stand the brutal midday rays you might be rewarded with uncluttered waves.

WHY HAWAII? THE CALL OF THE WILD

So why go to all the trouble of going to Hawaii just to subject yourself to so much possible trauma and tension? If you don't go, you'll never know.

All of the very best surfers in the world travel to Hawaii to find out just exactly how well their high regard for their ability holds up in the unflinching reality of the most consistently challenging surf arena in the world.

Hawaii lurks like a spider in a horribly efficient web that patiently waits to snare swells from all over the Pacific.

All storms send swells radiating outward, from horrendous winter tempests in the North Pacific to distant summer hurricanes off Mexico, cyclones in the South Pacific and fierce Antarctic storms that sweep past Australia and New Zealand. Hawaii's reefs snag these swells and force them to produce good waves all year long.

Years of exquisitely terrible excitement and adventure have confirmed Hawaii's extravagant claim to all of surfing's superlatives--most consistent surf, biggest waves, deepest tubes, fiercest crowds, hottest performances.

Almost nothing in life that is worth enjoying is very satisfying unless you experience it up close and personal. If you're really serious about your surfing, it's time to go beyond the magazines, movies and second-hand stories and find out what surfing Hawaii is really like.

Reputations are won, fame secured, fortunes made and legends born in Hawaii's sun-sparkled waves, and there is an electrical excitement in being part of it all, no matter how peripherally.

All surfing innovations, from new surfboard shapes to amazing maneuvers, are brought to Hawaii for validation before being embraced or discarded.

Despite all the crowds, hassles and hazards in Hawaii's waves, the sheer power of the physical beauty of these islands can make this a dream visit.

One day as you take yet another leisurely stroll along the beach you'll suddenly marvel that the ocean can clothe itself in so many different shades of aqua, turquoise, blue and green. On glassy days it's like surfing in blue-tinted crystal.

The simplest sensations can be overwhelming: enjoy the feel of the coarse or fine sand particles squishing between your toes, and be blinded by the shocking white foam as it washes up around your ankles.

Peel off your neoprene skin and savor the pure delight of feeling warm sun and water as you surf in the middle of winter without the maddening constrictions of a wetsuit.

If one visit isn't enough and you find yourself becoming addicted to Hawaii surf vacations, you just might find yourself in the lineup between sets pondering how the same water can be warm in winter and cool in the summer.

Enjoy the thrill of getting acquainted with a new lineup and the exciting shoreline view from the waves, with strange valleys and mountains behind tropical foliage lining the white sandy shore.

Take time to lounge on the beach between sessions or when conditions are way beyond your ability and watch the greatest surf show on Earth as the planet's hottest surfers set the waves ablaze.

Surfers come from all over the world to squeeze some fresh Hawaiian juice out of Hawaii's waves. Summertime Waikiki can satisfy. Photo: Warren Bolster

3

STAYING ALIVE

The moving target is hard to hit

Except for the nooks and crannies on the Outer Islands, crowds are a fact of life in Hawaii, and you alone can determine how safe your surf session will be.

The main thing is to stay out of the way. Don't drop in on anyone unless you are prepared to get a surfboard lodged in your back. When you're caught inside by a surprise set or are stroking for your life on the way back to the lineup, it's your responsibility to get out of the rider's path.

The only way to be certain you won't be dissected by a surfer jamming to make the wave is to go where he's already been, not where he wants to go. Paddle for the white water and take the trip through the industrial-strength washing machine comforted by the thought that not only did you avoid spoiling someone's ride, but you escaped getting your body cut in half.

Always paddle around the breaking waves and avoid the impulse to take shortcuts and forage for inside waves on your way back to the lineup. When the inevitable set comes and you're racing some rider for the shoulder, you'll be dismayed to learn that most surfers would rather try to make the wave than miss you.

Are you really experienced?

So you think you're ready for Hawaii's waves? You take pride in the 2 minutes you can hold your breath in a pool, and how you swim 2 miles a day. Well, the next time your local shorebreak hits 5 feet, sprint 50 yards and dive into the set of the day. Now how long does that precious lungful of air last?

Imagine getting pounded by a megadeath set a quarter of a mile from the beach after paddling furiously for (or to avoid) a wave. Leashes snap, boards break and if you aren't an incredible roughwater swimmer, your surf trip to Hawaii can become a disaster of savage beatings from waves and frantic battles with churning rip currents as the shore quickly fades into the distance.

Hawaii is a dangerous place to surf. Each year there are at least 325 surf-related injuries serious enough to require professional medical treatment, and countless other mishaps where surfers crawl home to lick their wounds and doctor themselves.

For visitor or local, expert or novice, the surf is the great equalizer that pummels everyone with equal savagery.

In a grim two-year period two California pro surfers died in the waves while practicing for a surf contest.

One died in medium-sized surf at Pipeline when he attempted an unwise maneuver and the wave dashed him against the coral.

The other unfortunate pro was surfing a small day at Rocky Point when the rip took him down to Gas Chambers and his cord became snagged on a rock. Before he could free himself, a set came in and he drowned.

Sometimes years of experience and familiarity with one spot aren't enough to save you from trouble.

Gerry Lopez has clocked more time inside Pipeline's tubes than most people spend in a grocery checkout line, and he has Pipeline's many moods totally wired. Yet while he was riding the white water to shore one day the wave took his board and shoved it into a very delicate area, nearly killing Lopez and forcing the Pipeline master to endure months of painful therapy.

Nor is the menacing surf zone of the North Shore the only place where trouble lurks to leap out and grab you. While the waves in Waikiki are certainly less fierce, the overwhelming crowds make it another deadly arena.

One teen-age Hawaiian lad who had spent his entire life surfing and swimming in Town's tame waves was shoved into an underwater cave at Queens and drowned before lifeguards could rescue him.

Give Lady Luck a hand

It's useless to try to control the ocean's wild power, and bad luck will grab you no matter how frantically you try to dodge its rough grasp, but there is much you can do to keep them from ganging up and mauling you during your surf session.

Everyone needs to survive at least one horrid misadventure where the waves are in such complete control that imminent death is not only probable, but a possible relief.

A session of nightmarish proportions establishes your personal parameters, helps you savor life more fully and makes other less consequential days seem easy to manage.

But if you exceed the limits of your ability too often, eventually you won't make it back to the beach.

Before you plunge recklessly into the waves, take a few moments to prepare your mind and body. See how often the sets come in, and how many waves each set is packing. Time the cleanup and closeout sets, and notice where the rip is running and how rapid it is.

And while you're waiting to see who is ripping and who is cringing, do some stretches before the waves and your own radical maneuvers wrench your limbs into painful contortions.

Focus your thoughts and project yourself out in the waves for some mind-surfing. Are you shredding? Are you getting pounded? Are 50 of the world's hottest surfers out there sucking up every wave like a herd of Hoover vacuums stuck on high speed?

If it looks from the beach like you're probably in for a miserable time out there, it might be a good day to just watch the action, or go foraging for a less crowded or safer spot.

If you do head out and the first big set has its way with you and escorts you roughly to the beach, perhaps the ocean is doing you a favor before you have a chance to really get hurt.

Current affairs

If your ultimate nightmare comes true before your unbelieving eyes and the waves snap your board or treacherously break your cord just as the set of the day is looming on the horizon, don't panic. The beach is your goal, and the waves will take you there if you give them a chance.

Don't swim out to sea, and don't try to dive under the waves to avoid the impact. That will just take you beyond the surf for a long, slow trip to Kauai or the Philippines in the current.

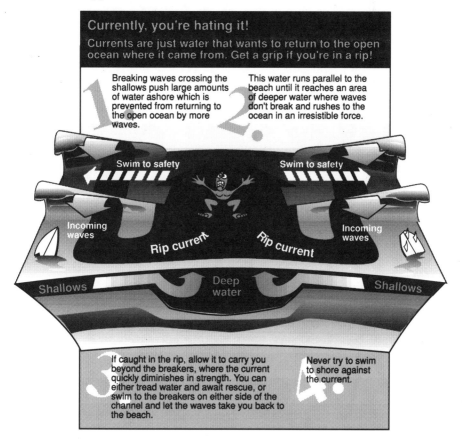

Currently, you're hating it!
Currents are just water that wants to return to the open ocean where it came from. Get a grip if you're in a rip!

1. Breaking waves crossing the shallows push large amounts of water ashore which is prevented from returning to the open ocean by more waves.

2. This water runs parallel to the beach until it reaches an area of deeper water where waves don't break and rushes to the ocean in an irresistible force.

Swim to safety

Swim to safety

Incoming waves

Incoming waves

Rip current

Rip current

Shallows

Deep water

Shallows

3. If caught in the rip, allow it to carry you beyond the breakers, where the current quickly diminishes in strength. You can either tread water and await rescue, or swim to the breakers on either side of the channel and let the waves take you back to the beach.

4. Never try to swim to shore against the current.

7

In smaller waves, try to bodysurf the white water to the beach. In big waves, duck underwater and point your feet toward the beach for a subsurface sleigh ride to shore.

If you're already in the rip being dragged out to sea, just head for the breaking waves on either side of the rip and let the waves' energy take you to the beach. The natural impulse to swim straight to shore through the rip is one of those inexplicable suicidal impulses that helps keep humans from overrunning the entire planet. Swimming against the rip will drain your energy as you struggle against a force strong enough to exhaust a shark.

HELP..

If drowning seems preferable to swimming toward the waves on either side of you as the rip carries you seaward, then just let the rip carry you beyond the breakers. The current will quickly dissipate and you can tread water until you are rescued, or swim to an easy landing site.

Talk to the angels

Always have a chat with the lifeguards before you surf. These guardian angels have seen every horrible thing the ocean can do to people, and a few seemingly idiotic questions can save you heaps of misery.

The lifeguards all surf or bodysurf, and are vast repositories of ocean wisdom. They can point out all the hazardous rips, rocky reefs and tricky waves that you will otherwise learn about through painful experience.

Keeping a cool head

If you can think of the turbulent tumbling of a wipeout as an aqua-massage by the ocean, it can be a fairly enjoyable sensation. But after the wave is through stretching your ligaments and tendons and you can finally climb your cord back to the surface for that precious breath of air, keep an arm over your head. It would be a real shock to have your sweet gulp of air interrupted by a blow to your head from your board after the wave has finished tossing it around.

Feeding frenzy

Something terrible happens to the human ego when cameras appear in the water and on the beach. Suddenly, your best friend is stuffing you in the pit for a chance at celluloid immortality.

The sight of cameras cluttering the sand and clogging the waves is a major clue that a dangerous situation exists. Flee, before your own ego swells and lures you into the lineup as you feverishly disregard your brain's sensible advice that the photogs aren't likely to waste precious film on you.

It's a good idea to surf with friends. Not only is it more fun to have someone you know hooting for your rides, but you can block for each other in a crowded lineup, and help each other out of tough situations.

And if the worst occurs, there will be someone to tell of your last great ride, which is immensely preferable to an anonymous death alone.

The presence of photogs at Pipeline produces the same effect in the lineup as tossing a wounded kitten to a pack of pit bulls. Photo: Warren Bolster

DEADLY CREATURES

The bad boys

The fiercest predators you will ever encounter in Hawaiian waters are the surfers. Something amazing happens when you take the greediest, most aggressive surfers from the mainland, Brazil, Japan and Australia and plop them into Hawaii's waves. The intensity level escalates unbearably until it seems the surrounding molecules will spontaneously combust.

It appears that everyone is driven insane by the thought that the surf photographers are going to make them famous if only they can prove themselves by outsurfing the top pros.

Many surfers are grappling with inner demons that taunt them by questioning whether they can perform in Hawaii's surf, and the waves churn with frenzied activity as they seek to prove themselves.

These hyper-amped surfers are much more of a threat to your safety than any of God's sea creatures.

UH... BRAH?

Things that bite

As you might expect of such a warm semitropical ocean, there are plenty of sharks going about their business in Hawaii. Most of them aren't interested in you, though it is a solid rush to catch a glimpse of white- and black-tipped reef sharks, gray reef sharks and hammerheads.

You don't even want to be within yelling distance if someone spots a tiger shark, though.

They are easily identified by a blunt nose, wide, square mouth brimming with serrated teeth and gray/brown body with stripes. These guys are the biggest predators in Hawaiian waters, some reaching 18 feet.

After Billy Weaver was killed off Lanikai in 1959, tigers bit more than a few divers, surfers and swimmers, but didn't kill anyone. Then in November, 1992, tigers began a spate of attacks, some fatal, that still has marine biologists puzzled.

The attacks eventually slowed, then stopped. There will be more, and it's best to remember that the ocean is the sharks' home and you are just a visitor, an especially slow and helpless visitor at that.

You can increase your chances of never seeing a tiger shark by not surfing in murky rain-runoff water, and by avoiding areas where there are dead fish or other animals in the water.

It has been suggested that tiger sharks hunt near shore at night and head for deeper water during the day, but researchers haven't confirmed that, so it's not clear whether it is worth it to miss the prime surfing times of dawn and dusk.

Seven million people enter Hawaii's ocean each year and never encounter a shark. But if you do, some surfers have sent sharks fleeing by punching them in the snout, which is filled with sensitive nerve endings. While a shark's muscular body is covered with sandpaper-rough skin, its eyes are especially vulnerable to a gouge. Evacuate the area slowly but purposefully, without panicking and splashing.

Slithery varmints

Central American sea snakes occasionally take a free trip to Hawaii, carried by open ocean currents, but they are as rare as an empty wave.

You can identify them by their sleek black body and yellow belly. If you see one, be careful who you tell. Most people will either think you deranged or a liar, although the occasional marine biologist might listen to your tale with interest.

Hawaii's reefs are fairly swarming with eels, but unless you stick your feet or hands in their hidey-holes and stress them, these toothsome critters won't bother you.

However, they are tenacious when provoked, and if one gets ahold of you the best escape tactic is to relax until the eel lets loose to get a better grip. That's your opening to either grab it behind the head, or set the water afire as you blaze away from your tormentor.

Their rather vicious set of teeth curve inward, so if you panic and try to pull one off you'll be in for the same futile, nasty struggle as if you tried to yank a determined pit bull off your arm.

11

Pointy things

The local sea life you will have the greatest chance of interacting with, to your everlasting detriment, are sea urchins. There are many varieties of these bottom dwellers, and in places the reef is lousy with their sharp spines. Although some types will cause you more misery than others, they are all to be avoided.

Fortunately, that's easy to do. Just resist the impulse to walk on the reef, and you'll never meet these guys.

If you do tread on them, don't try to remove the spines that remain embedded in your skin. They are brittle and have barbs that make them impossible to extract. Keep the wound clean with isopropyl alcohol and hydrogen peroxide, and time will dissolve the spines. If the wound becomes infected, it's time to see a doctor before it gets out of control.

Coral is everywhere, and luckily so, for without coral we wouldn't have many ridable waves. But much of the coral is sharp and alive. Even if you

master the art of the shallow-penetration dive during a wipeout, you are certain to get scraped eventually.

Just make sure you extract all the coral particles from your wound, and keep it clean with the same steadfast duo of isopropyl alcohol and hydrogen peroxide. If you don't keep on it, the streptococcus bacteria so common here will turn your wound into an angry red volcano erupting molten pus.

Stinging blobs

Hawaii's waters are regularly visited by flotillas of jellyblobs whose stings, while not fatal, can painfully earn your undivided attention. One severe sting can cause you to sullenly meditate on the mystery of what possible benefit they could provide that would earn them their miserable place in the grand scheme of things.

Surely a benevolent creator wouldn't devise a creature that existed solely to torment surfers? No shore is safe from the irksome Portuguese man-o-war, though surfers on the windward side of each island are afflicted most often because these jellyfish blow with the breeze.

An air-filled, clear bladder pulls a dangerous line of tentacles on a ride through the ocean wherever the wind takes it. Only surfers trying to find some fun in waves where the wind is blowing sideshore or onshore will be afflicted by man-o-wars.

Although incredibly painful, man-o-war stings aren't fatal, though the thought of stinging tentacles lashing your eyes as you push through a wave is ghastly to contemplate.

The translucent, bobbing blue bubble is innocent-looking and easy to spot, but it trails long tentacles that can wrap around your body and deliver a sting painful enough to make you forget your girlfriend's name. If these blue lassos of misery rope you, quickly pull off the stinging tentacles and paddle to the beach to scrub off any remaining tentacles with sand.

Meat tenderizer will help neutralize the remaining toxin, and if none is available, urine will do the trick. People who are hypersensitive to the toxin should be quickly taken to an emergency room.

Eventually the wind and waves dump these little devils on the shore, and the bubble makes a most satisfying pop as you vengefully stomp the man-o-wars helplessly stranded on the beach.

A more villainous blob that is impossible to spot is the box jellyfish, the less lethal cousin to the dreaded and frequently fatal sea wasp that haunts Australia's tropical waters.

Hawaii's box jellyfish delivers an agonizing sting that in many cases deserves quick medical attention from lifeguards or other emergency medical personnel. A usually effective home remedy is to treat the sting with a paste made of vinegar and meat tenderizer, one that contains papaya enzymes.

These translucent pests slink underwater through the lineup disguised so cleverly that they are as impossible to spot as fist-sized chunks of ice in the waves. They are most common on the south and west shores of Oahu, but because they travel just under the surface they can show up on any beach in the state to wash in and out with the tides in a vast undulating blanket of stinging blobs. Whether you paddle in when the surfers around you start getting zapped depends on how good the waves are.

When the waves wash them ashore, the box jellyfish are stripped of their cloak of invisibility by the sand that clings to their clear bodies, making them easy to spot. A quick stroll along the beach will let you know whether the fleet is in, and help you decide just how good the waves really are.

THE OCEAN IN MOTION

Having a swell time

If you surf in Hawaii often enough during the winter you will eventually be treated to one of the most exquisitely terrifying events in all of surfing: the arrival of a new swell.

While many new swells sneak ashore under the cover of darkness, others come muscling ashore in the full light of day, with dangerous results.

You will be out enjoying a harmless little 3- to 5-foot day at your favorite spot when you are stupefied to spot a giant set looming on the horizon. After paddling frantically to escape these rogue monsters, if you're lucky you'll be left sitting far from shore watching the lineup

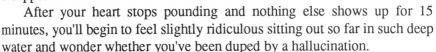

disappear under a maelstrom of white water.

After your heart stops pounding and nothing else shows up for 15 minutes, you'll begin to feel slightly ridiculous sitting out so far in such deep water and wonder whether you've been duped by a hallucination.

After paddling cautiously in and riding a few more fun 5-footers, your furtive seaward glances will spot another, larger rogue set and your race for the horizon will begin again.

Eventually these scout waves will be reinforced by the main army of the swell.

Don't worry; until you are overwhelmed by the full wave invasion you can take delight in the thrill of paddling for your life, secure in the knowledge that when you decide it's time to go in, the waves will be happy to quickly escort you to the beach.

Seasons blowing in the wind

Although most people think of Hawaii as being pleasantly trapped in an eternal spring, that's not true. Surfers are especially aware of the subtle physical differences that mark the changing seasons in Hawaii because the wave and wind patterns provide the most obvious seasonal clues.

Even though Hawaii's surf is a slave to predictable storm systems that bring huge northwest winter swells to the north shores and fun summer south swells to the south shores, there are unseasonal swells that you can pounce on for uncrowded waves.

The North Pacific storms that batter the north shores all winter continue through the summer, though with much less vigor. Similarly, the Southern Hemisphere storms can crank out unexpected south swells during the winter months and let some good waves slip past Hawaii's usually vigilant wave watchers.

By staying alert and constantly checking all shores for waves, you can frequently snatch some empty waves, a trick that is as exciting as stealing treasure from under the dragon's snout.

You can pretty much assume that if you come to Hawaii, there will be waves. But keeping a sharp eye on conditions around you will make the difference between scoring good waves and being tormented by surfers telling you about the good waves when you show up a day late and a dollar short.

It's difficult to comprehend how something so invisible can have such a dramatic effect on your life, but the wind determines whether the waves are visions of delight or delusions of despair. Hawaii's wind patterns are simple and predictable, and by understanding them you can be on top of the wave conditions.

Trade winds blow 70 percent of the time in the Hawaiian Islands, which can be good or bad, depending on which shore you want to surf. "Trade winds" is a slippery term that describes a wide variety of winds from the north-northeast--great if you're surfing on the south shores--all the way to straight easterly winds, prime for the north shores.

The rest of the year the wind blows 10 percent each from the southeast, southwest and northwest quadrants, which makes alert surfers smile as they contemplate riding clean waves at spots usually shredded by the trades, such as the windward and northwest shores of all islands.

15

Winter usually has the cleanest waves, because the trades blow most often during the summer, leaving the winter months blessed with many glassy days.

When cold fronts come blowing in to the Hawaiian Islands they bring a special series of winds that sharp surfers can use to their advantage. As the front advances it sucks up moist air from the south, and for about a day southwesterly kona winds will blow offshore on the north and northeast shores. When the advancing swell or the lingering swell from a previous storm are greeted by these southwest winds, the resulting waves are a pure delight.

As the front passes through the islands, the wind shifts until it becomes northwest or north, a boon to the spots on the east and southeast shores.

Southwesterly kona winds are also produced by local low-pressure systems called kona storms. These ill-tempered beasts roam around the islands for days, flinging lightning bolts and dumping buckets of rain. Also in their arsenal are southwest winds, which have windward surfers grinning as they wax their boards in anticipation of surfing seldom-smooth waves in their own backyard.

It is a rare and wonderful event when you can please everyone, but that happens fairly often in Hawaii. Whenever the trades disappear and no other wind system appears to take their place, the Islands are placed in the gentle grasp of variable winds.

This means that early in the morning and late in the afternoon the wind will be offshore on every shore on every island. If there is any kind of swell hitting, surfers will be treated to clean conditions. And if several swells are launching a simultaneous assault, Hawaii will be surrounded by waves, and surfers will have no choice but to surf their way out. This usually happens in the fall and spring, when late or early south swells team up with late or early north swells, and surfers go crazy trying to decide which excellent surf spots to terrorize.

The source of this magical benevolence is the different ways that the ocean and land deal with solar heat. The ocean absorbs heat and remains at a fairly constant temperature day or night, while the temperamental land heats up quickly during the day and cools off quickly at night.

When the land is cool, it creates a high-pressure zone where cool air flows out to sea, producing a gentle offshore land breeze that sculpts the waves to perfection early in the morning and late in the afternoon. As the sun heats the land during the day, the cooler ocean air flows ashore to replace the rising hot land air, and sea breezes flaw the previously flawless waves.

The sight of early morning smooth waves caressed by a gentle offshore breeze produces in surfers the kind of overwhelming emotional response that their human lovers can seldom hope to inspire.

Singing the no-surf blues

You can always take a chance and travel to some remote part of the world, and your gamble might pay off with waves good enough to make your body twitch years later at the memory.

But if you endure all the hardships of third world travel and the waves don't show up, you'll be stuck in the bush tormented by some tropical disease or trapped in some horrid wasteland, stupefied by boredom.

So you've planned your surf trip to Hawaii with maddening precision using wave and weather reports from the past 30 years to find the perfect time for surf so you can maximize your precious vacation time. Incredibly, the ocean has fallen asleep, and even torching your friend's new big-wave gun on the beach at midnight doesn't bring any surf.

Or even worse, a 20-foot swell arrives hustled ashore by howling onshore winds. Don't despair, Hawaii has heaps of diversions to keep you amused until the next swell arrives to save your sanity.

Waikiki in the summertime and in the dead of winter is swarming with interesting specimens of humanity from around the world, and the beaches overflow with vacationers by day, and the nightclubs are jammed at night.

Waikiki Beach is possibly the finest hangout spot in the world. Just find a strategic spot, preferably with shade during the day, and arm yourself with enough food and drink to last a few hours. Eventually every amazing variety of the human species will pass before your unbelieving eyes, to your vast entertainment.

With so many surfers from foreign lands attracted to Hawaii, surfless days are a good time to seek out the Aussies, Japanese, Brazilians and others and chat them up about the surf in their homeland. Not only can you pick up some excellent tips for your next surf trip, you just might make a friend for life.

It would tax the mental faculties of some very imaginative people to think of a place that lures more of the world's top surfers into the same place at the same time than Oahu's North Shore during the winter.

Every surfer you've ever admired will eventually show up at some time on the North Shore each winter. The trick is to ferret out their hiding places so you can talk to them, meet them or just watch them so you can impress your friends back home. It's always revealing to hear these performers detail the excruciating amount of practice, discipline and commitment necessary to excel at their sport.

Luckily, although they inhabit a performance plane unimaginably higher than anything you can ever hope to attain, these surf stars are only human and have to leave their lairs to perform their daily chores.

A good place to begin stargazing is Foodland across from the Sunset Beach Fire Station. The surf shops in Haleiwa are also good hunting grounds.

One prime hangout is the compound near Sunset Beach that contains Kammie's Market, the Sunset Beach Surf Shop, Sunset Diner's and a self-service laundry, which together accommodate almost any need that a surfer might have. Eventually, every surf star in the world passes through this celebrity trap.

Many top surfers cope with the stress of no surf by bashing tennis balls about. It's a good plan to haunt the courts at the Turtle Bay Hilton, Sunset Beach Elementary School or Waialua Recreation Center until the surfing luminaries show up to do battle.

When the surf stars head for the Neighbor Islands it's too easy for them to vanish, only to reappear in the waves. The only guaranteed place to find them is on the best waves during the exceptional swells.

LIVING WITHOUT WALLS

The choices of lodging in Hawaii run from expensive beachfront luxury to squalid trolls' dens shared by a dozen surfers. Your budget and temperament will help you select the right shelter, with the help of a good travel agent. But probably the least expensive dwelling that puts you right at the ocean's edge is a tent.

Each island has numerous fine state and county oceanfront campgrounds that are yours free or for a modest fee after you obtain a permit from the appropriate government agency (see page 155).

Camping will save you heaps of money, and force you to immerse yourself in the beautiful Hawaiian environment. You'll also get to know the locals well, and appreciate them as generous, fun people.

If you're camping it's best to have a car as a sort of mobile strongbox to store your precious possessions when you're hunting for waves.

Summers are mostly free from the Hawaii camper's biggest enemy: rain. Each winter is different, as some are blessed with fine weather and only a few damp days, while others are so wet that mold starts growing on you if you pause to rest for even a few seconds.

The weather systems that bring rain are simple and few. Cold fronts bring giant waves and fast-moving squalls and are preceded and followed by days of perfect weather. These are usually only a slight nuisance.

Low-pressure systems that develop near the Hawaiian Islands are called kona storms, and these miserable soggy beasts are slow-moving storms that aimlessly loiter around the islands with heavy deluges and spectacular displays of thunder and lightning. It is during kona storms that surfers are most at risk of being bashed by their mates driven mad by days of hearing raindrops spatter on the tent top or tin roof of their rental house.

This is no time to be sheltered from the elements by only your tent's thin membrane, and the remedy is to break camp and rent a room somewhere until the storm blows over.

But the warm Hawaiian rain shouldn't prevent anyone from enjoying one of life's sublime pleasures: waking up in a tent to the sound of waves breaking nearby.

DON'T BE BORED WITH YOUR BOARD

If you're coming to Hawaii in the summer, any board will do, from supertanker to subsurface whippersnapper. Summer waves are usually so forgiving that whatever you choose to ride will work just fine. If a bull of a swell comes in and makes you lose faith in your equipment, you can always rent a board until the dying swell eases your crisis of confidence.

In the winter, your life can depend on your choice of equipment. Your favorite beachbreak lip banger is just going to betray you in Hawaii and set you up for the painful revelation that all surfboards are not created equal.

If you're dead set on surfing your homeboy boards in some serious winter waves, you'll need at least two boards. Bring one board that is a demon in double overhead waves, and another that will perform in overhead and smaller waves.

The absolute best way to make sure that your board survives the stress tests conducted by the slaves of the goddess of destruction who handle airline baggage is to wrap it in plastic bubbles and pack it in a cardboard box. The domestic U.S. airlines charge $30 per oversized package, so by squeezing two boards into the same box you can save yourself an additional $30.

But to really save money and trauma, you might consider buying boards made in Hawaii for Hawaii's waves. Your first savings will be the $60 round-trip baggage fee. The next savings will be the cost of replacing your broken board.

Hawaii's waves are infamous pranksters that delight in snapping your cord and sending your board on a free float to Kauai and beyond. They are also muscle-flexing fools that break boards with no apparent effort. Why spend so much money importing a board destined to let you down or end up as fiberglass kindling littering the beach?

The world's wisest shaping gurus test their brainstorms in Hawaii's waves, and while even the top pros have to wait in line for a new board from the hottest shapers, Hawaii is filled with good used boards at reasonable prices.

Once you finally struggle to escape the clutches of the rip, it eases your sense of loss as you gather the shards of your broken board to realize that you bought it cheap. All year long surfers are upgrading their quivers, and deals abound. Many pros jettison their entire quiver at the beginning and end of their visit and aren't looking for top dollar when they sell them.

And if your previously ridden Hawaii board survives your Island misadventures you can always sell it before you leave, or take it home to familiar waters to see if it really was the board that kept you from surfing up to your expectations in Hawaii.

The inevitable dings, wrenched fins and snapped boards are only a minor setback. If ability or circum-stances force you to make your own repairs, material is widely available at most hardware stores and surf shops.

Hawaii's fiberglass wizards can return a board almost to its pre-disaster condition if you've got enough money. Prices vary widely, so shop around.

IF YOU HAD WINGS

The ultimate situation is to have your own car waiting as soon as your plane touches down so you can jump in and immediately start sniffing around for waves.

But it's possible to still track down your share of waves without a car. It's just a matter of deciding in advance where you want to hunt, and where you want to stay.

If you decide to stalk the warmer, less threatening summer swells, you can walk to at least 35 surf spots from anywhere in Waikiki. You can double your foraging area by renting a moped, an option for many younger surfers who don't have the necessary credit card to rent a car.

If tracking the wild winter waves is your game, you can reach most of the North Shore's prime locations on foot if you're staying in Haleiwa, the Chun's Reef area, Rocky Point or Sunset Beach. Once again, a bicycle or moped can open up a world of different spots to you.

Having an innocent face or a lot of friends can get you to the waves and spare you the expense and hassles of having a car.

With an innocent face you can hitchhike to the waves with a reasonable chance of getting rides. And with a lot of friends someone is bound to let you come along, as long as you're willing to surf where the group decides, no matter how hopeless the waves.

But to effectively stalk the elusive uncrowded Hawaiian wave, a car is essential. Most of the uncrowded waves can be reached only by car, and these secluded surf spots provide the most rewarding surfing experiences.

If your surf trip is going to be fairly short, a rental car is your best bet. This means you'll need a credit card, as almost no company will let you rent a car without one.

Many airlines offer a fly-and-drive package, which is a pretty good deal, and renting at a weekly rate will save you money. All the companies are competitive, and one canny trick is to have a car reserved from the company with the best rate that your travel agent can secure, then use the phone book once you arrive and search for a better rate with the numerous lesser-known local firms.

If you're lucky enough to have a long, leisurely surfari in Hawaii, you can buy a beachmobile at a reasonable rate and sell it when you leave, presuming there is anything left.

This necessitates one of life's most disagreeable ordeals: a visit to the bureaucratic gnomes who exist only to torment their fellow man. But it's worth the unpleasantness of a wasted day battling with the forces of mediocrity for auto registration and no-fault insurance to end up with a magic carpet that will take you anywhere on a whim.

Your mobile status will also earn you a lot of new friends pumping up your ego as they slyly hustle you for a ride to the waves.

The best places to find out about deals on wheels are in the daily and community newspapers, on the bulletin boards outside the supermarkets, and by talking to other surfers.

You can actually feel smug about saving a doomed vehicle from premature death by recycling a car that is pinging toward its last mile as it valiantly struggles to get you to the waves. Surfers are so hard on cars that they are usually the bottom feeders in the great automotive food chain, and the end of the line for most cars.

OAHU GETS ALL THE BREAKS

Oahu is blessed with the greatest concentration of quality surf spots in the Hawaiian Islands. Most surfers can't cope with such a bewildering variety of good spots, and spend hours driving aimlessly from spot to spot, hopelessly unable to decide which waves to ride.

Unfortunately, Oahu is also cursed with the greatest concentration of adept wave snatchers in the known surfing world. When you add the fluctuating numbers of visiting surfers, you have a seascape of exceptional surf spots swarming with ravening surfers.

From the winter's harrowing waves on the North Shore and summer's fun South Shore surf to the splendid overlapping swells of spring and fall, Oahu has every surfing experience you can possibly imagine.

KAUAI GETS IT FROM ALL SIDES

Only 23 minutes from Oahu by plane, Kauai might as well be in another galaxy.

Here you will find the true exotic Hawaiian surfing experience, filled with friendly locals and uncrowded waves breaking in a breathtaking setting.

Kauai takes all swells and embraces them with its round shape, letting each swell wrap onto several shores simultaneously and enhancing the effect of the swell.

For all its rustic charm, Kauai lacks even the suggestion of the nighttime entertainment that makes Oahu so lively. When the waves decide to play coy and not show their faces, alternate activities consist mainly of hiking, diving and fishing. Actually, when you think about it, those are quite fine ways to pass the time.

Your choices of accommodations range from a rental house or condo on the north shore or in Princeville to hotels and condos in Poipu on the south shore. A good travel agent should be able to find you a fine deal.

MAUI HAS MILES OF SMILES

Maui is a surfer's dream that includes waves that can challenge surfers and sailboarders beyond anything they have ever encountered, as well as friendly peaks suitable for beginners.

Although you might have to put in some brain-numbing miles to reach the best surf, with a little patience and luck Maui will treat you to a gratifying variety of surfing experiences.

Maui's coastline faces enough directions that there is always a wave breaking somewhere that is calling your name. Unfortunately, the various surf zones are so spread out you can develop white-line hallucinations cruising from Hookipa on the northeast shore to check out a rumored swell at Honolua on the northwest shore.

But after a good session you'll be willing to endure any hardship for another dose of pleasure.

Although more crowded than Kauai or the Big Island, the crowds on Maui never begin to approach the frenzied hordes that terrorize Oahu's waves. Although Lahaina and the Kaanapali resorts are the closest Maui can come to providing the nocturnal amusements of Waikiki, the simple diversions of diving, hiking and exploring more than make up for this lack.

THE BIG ISLAND SUFFERS GROWING PAINS

The Big Island has the dubious distinction of being one of the few places on the planet where Mother Nature is taking back some of the surf spots she so generously bestowed upon us.

Madame Pele has sent a river of molten lava to cover the waves at Drainpipes and other spots in Kaimu Bay, devastating the surfing community of Kalapana.

Anyone who has ever sampled the delights of Drainpipes' powerful rights and the other fine spots in the bay will be saddened by the destruction of these waves, which now exist only in memory.

The Big Island still has many excellent surf spots, though they are spread so far apart and many are so inaccessible that you will have to invest a great effort to get a good sampling of the Big Island's waves.

But along the way you will see every landscape and environment known to man, from snow-capped volcanic peaks and cool upland pastures to desolate lava fields, steamy jungles and isolated tree-lined bays, where you might be the only person surfing.

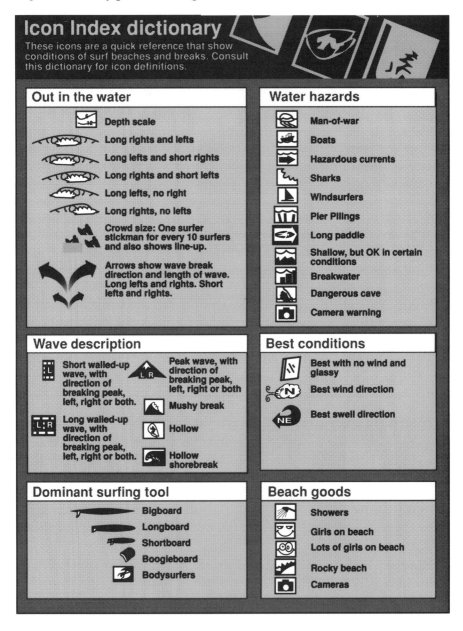

Icon Index dictionary

These icons are a quick reference that show conditions of surf beaches and breaks. Consult this dictionary for icon definitions.

Out in the water

- Depth scale
- Long rights and lefts
- Long lefts and short rights
- Long rights and short lefts
- Long lefts, no right
- Long rights, no lefts
- Crowd size: One surfer stickman for every 10 surfers and also shows line-up.
- Arrows show wave break direction and length of wave. Long lefts and rights. Short lefts and rights.

Water hazards

- Man-of-war
- Boats
- Hazardous currents
- Sharks
- Windsurfers
- Pier Pilings
- Long paddle
- Shallow, but OK in certain conditions
- Breakwater
- Dangerous cave
- Camera warning

Wave description

- Short walled-up wave, with direction of breaking peak, left, right or both.
- Long walled-up wave, with direction of breaking peak, left, right or both.
- Peak wave, with direction of breaking peak, left, right or both
- Mushy break
- Hollow
- Hollow shorebreak

Best conditions

- Best with no wind and glassy
- Best wind direction
- Best swell direction

Dominant surfing tool

- Bigboard
- Longboard
- Shortboard
- Boogieboard
- Bodysurfers

Beach goods

- Showers
- Girls on beach
- Lots of girls on beach
- Rocky beach
- Cameras

24

CHAPTER 1

OAHU
GETS ALL THE
BREAKS!

This is the master map. Consult this map for direction and breakdown of blow-up areas to be showcased in the following pages.

HAWAIIAN ISLANDS

Niihau ◇ Kauai

Oahu 🦅 Molokai

Lanai ◗🦀 Maui

Kahoolawe

Hawaii

Kahuku Point

North Shore, Breaks 14-25

Sunset Beach

Kahuku

Laie

Kaena Point

Haleiwa

Farrington Hwy.

Mokuleia

East Shore, Breaks 26-29

Kualoa Point

Kapuh Point

Makaha

Wahiawa

Waianae

Mililani

Kaneohe Bay

Mokapu Peninsula

West Shore, Breaks 10-13

Maili Point

Waipahu

Pearl City

Kaneohe

Kailua

Kahe Point

Pearl Harbor

Likelike Hwy.

Pali Hwy.

Waimanalo

Southeast Shore, Breaks 30-33

Ewa Beach

Honolulu

Makapuu Point

Barbers Point

Mamala Bay

Waikiki

Hanauma Bay

Honolulu Airport

South Shore, Breaks 1-9

Diamond Head

Koko Head

0 Miles 5

0 Kilometers 8

N

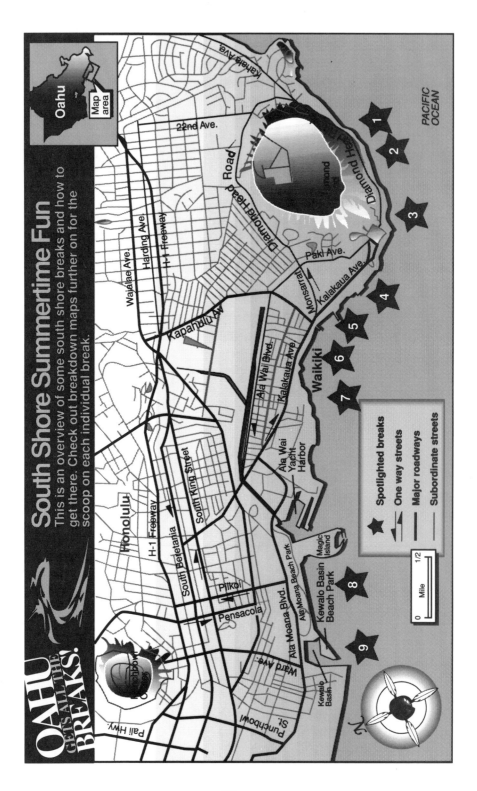

OAHU GETS ALL THE BREAKS!

South Shore Summertime Fun

This is an overview of some south shore breaks and how to get there. Check out breakdown maps further on for the scoop on each individual break.

Oahu

Map area

PACIFIC OCEAN

Diamond Head Road

Diamond Head

22nd Ave.

Kahela Ave.

Road

Harding Ave.

Waialae Ave.

H-1 Freeway

Paki Ave.

Monsarrat

Kalakaua Ave.

Kapahulu Av

Waikiki

Ala Wai Blvd.

Kalakaua Ave.

Ala Wai Yacht Harbor

Honolulu

H-1 Freeway

South King Street

Piikoi

South Beretania

Pensacola

Magic Island

Kewalo Basin Beach Park

Ala Moana Beach Park

Ala Moana Blvd.

Ward Ave.

Kewalo Basin

Punchbowl St.

Pali Hwy.

Spotlighted breaks
One way streets
Major roadways
Subordinate streets

0   Mile   1/2

26

Cliffs

Location: Off Diamond Head Park, below the lookout

Activities: Shortboard surfing, longboard surfing, windsurfing, bodyboarding

Wave: Fun, rippable rights and lefts, seldom hollow

Difficulty: Beginner, intermediate, expert

Prime time: Best April through September, breaks all year

Wave range: All swells with any south, 2-7 feet

Amenities: Parking, paved trail, shower, topless sunbathers on the beach

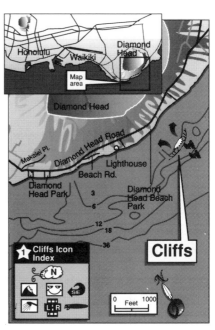

If you frequently surf at Cliffs beneath the imposing bulwark of Diamond Head, millions of people have watched you in action. The waves off Diamond Head are some of the most beautiful peaks in the state, and a constant parade of tourists pauses along Diamond Head Road to watch the action in the water. Add to that an endless stream of local residents passing by while jogging or riding bikes, or stopping to check the windsurfing conditions and surf possibilities, and you soon realize that those who surf these picturesque waves are well scrutinized.

The view along Diamond Head Road from above the waves can pierce your heart with its beauty, but distance and perspective act as a cosmetic on the waves. When you get close enough to become intimate with the waves, the surf is seldom as pretty as it appears from the lookout.

If the wind has elements of north in it, or is absent, then the waves at Cliffs can be as beautiful as they look. But the waves are usually marred by bumpy, lumpy faces and cross chop from a stiff sideshore breeze.

However, while the waves at Cliffs aren't usually picture perfect, they are consistent. Because of its prominent position on the South Shore, the reefs at the foot of Diamond Head hijack swells passing by from many directions and bend them into ridable waves. Swells with too much east or west in them to pay a visit to Honolulu's surf spots will focus on Diamond Head's reefs.

You'll have to spend a lot of hours bobbing in the water at Cliffs to find your way into any tubes, as the waves here are mostly high-performance, non-hollow walls. But the lineup is accommodating, with a variety of right and left peaks that can hold quite a crowd--which is fortunate, as this is a very accessible surf spot.

Another benefit is the channel on the west end of the reef, straight off from the shower on the beach, which makes it easy to get out to the waves. Unfortunately, it's the only channel in the lineup, and getting back out can become a vexing, vigorous bit of exercise when the swell is pumping.

Parking is simple; just find a spot along Diamond Head Road and head down the paved trail to the beach. Ripoffs are a problem, so it's best to take your car key with you and hide it on the beach.

When the wind really starts to howl and the waves start looking as appetizing as week-old pizza, it's time to head in before the windsurfers descend and drive you to the beach. Cliffs is a favorite sailing zone for world-class sailboarders, who not only snatch every wave in sight, but are hard to avoid as they jump waves while heading out to sea and ride waves on the way back in.

It's best to relinquish the waves to them and know that when the conditions are really clean for surfing, the sailboarders are stuck on the beach.

Whether you opt for the lefts or rights is a matter of personal preference, as each has its preferred swell direction and can sizzle on the right swell.

Just remember to smile as you surf, because someone is always watching.

Lighthouse

Location: Beneath Coast Guard Lighthouse at Diamond Head
Activities: Shortboard surfing, longboard surfing
Wave: Fast performance right, often hollow
Difficulty: Experts only
Prime time: Best April through September, breaks all year
Wave range: All swells with any south, 2-6 feet
Amenities: Parking, paved trail, shower, topless sunbathers on the beach

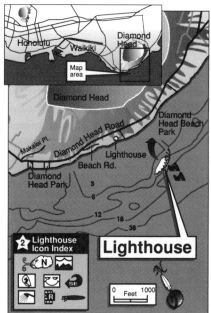

If you're looking for a fast, hollow right with an easy crowd, keep looking. You won't find it at Lighthouse, beneath the Diamond Head

Lookout. While the wave is ultra fast and can provide many fine trips to the tube, the crowd is anything but easy. These guys have been surfing here for years, and know every nuance of swell, wind and tide that affects the wave. They will outfox you every time and leave you wondering why you ever thought you knew how to surf.

The wave at Lighthouse always seems to beckon from the lookout, and while the wave gets bumpier the closer you get, it usually will provide a fun surf session. The view from the lineup is paradoxically relaxing and dynamic, with the looming bulk of Diamond Head in the background.

There's no telling how many surfers have sat in the lineup between waves and dreamed of owning the house within the Coast Guard Lighthouse complex atop the cliff. The supreme view of the ocean that is the prime pleasure of living in that house goes to the current commander of the area's Coast Guard, who is not likely to invite covetous surfers for a chat and to admire the scenery.

The reef is a bit more fickle than the reef at nearby Cliffs, and the swells line up less often, but Lighthouse is still one of the most consistent surf spots on the South Shore. The wind is the major factor that determines how good the surf is at Lighthouse, and with a hint of north or no wind the waves can be a delight.

The wave jumps up as it hits the shallow reef, and wedges into a gaping bowl on the inside section. If you and your board are still together after a late take-off, you can time your turn to launch into a quick trip to visit the tube monster. The local maestros divvy up these waves with a ruthless efficiency that is inspirational to watch, but intimidating to someone contemplating joining them in their feeding frenzy.

The reef is very sharp and quick to punish when you've made a mistake, and the longer you ride a wave, the greater your chance of impaling your board or body on the coral on the shallow inside section.

Still, there are peripheral moments, usually at dawn or dusk, when you can catch Lighthouse in a good mood and without other surfers snatching all the waves. Those are moments to savor.

Park along Diamond Head Road near the lookouts, walk down the paved trail and paddle straight out through the channel in front of the showers. Head toward Waikiki, and when you spot a sizzling, hollow right being lacerated by some unknown surfer, you're there. Paddling in is more of a problem, especially at low tide. If you head straight in, you might scrape your arms and board on the shallow coral. The best bet is to head back to the channel.

At medium or high tide you can ride your last wave until it is a tired little foamball, then keep stroking for the beach, and keep a lookout for the occasional coral head.

Suicides

Location: Off Diamond Head Park
Activities: Shortboard, longboard, bodyboard
Wave: Long performance left, hollow at low tide; short fun right
Difficulty: Average to intermediate
Prime time: April through September, breaks all year
Wave range: Best on southeast swell, fair on south and southwest, 2-4 feet
Amenities: Showers, nearby parking

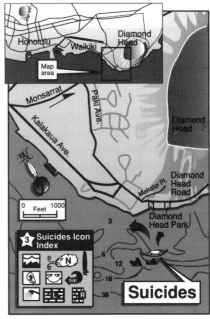

Suicides is a guaranteed good time, despite its rather alarming name. Although the reef can get nasty on the inside section at low tide, Suicides is a fun performance wave where an occasional tube makes a guest appearance.

The paddle out is easy at high tide, but at low tide a familiarity with the reef will save you from some painful nicks on your body and traumas to your board. Unwary surfers can get banged up a bit trying to find a safe passage through the coral labyrinth.

The best way to make it to the lineup is to watch the waves from the beach park, and locate the remains of an old pier at the end of the waves breaking left. When paddling out, stay about 30 yards to the left of the pier and you'll make it out unscathed.

Suicides' location on the town side of Diamond Head is a blessing that allows it to ensnare the waves from the full spectrum of south swells, from southeasterly wind swells to long-distance south and southwest swells. It can even pick up the occasional monster west-northwest winter swell, making it a very consistent surf playground.

Unfortunately, this location also means the trade winds blow sideshore here, and while Suicides isn't as fickle and wind-whipped as the surf spots off Diamond Head, it can get pretty ugly when the trades blow from the east.

But with glassy conditions or a touch of north in the wind, Suicides turns into a fine, long, rippable wave with a dedicated band of regulars that makes full use of the waves without being too difficult a crowd. Just make sure the fun wave doesn't lull you into riding into the exposed reef on the inside. On some of the longer lefts, there is the danger of continuing your ride into the exposed remains of an old pier.

Parking is a problem here, because there is none. At least not nearby, but if you cruise the surrounding streets you should be able to find a spot. If not, head back to Kapiolani Park and you should get lucky.

The tiny Diamond Head Park has plenty of shade, showers, grass, and a fine view of the waves. With enough time and provisions, you could spend the whole day surfing, watching others surf and stoking back into the lineup to surpass your previous efforts.

If that isn't sufficient motivation, there is usually the stirring sight of nearby topless sunbathers.

When any swell over 4 feet comes bruising ashore it overpowers the reef, turning Suicides into a confused mess of thrashing foam and sending the regulars elsewhere in search of a ridable wave.

If you paddle out on a day when the crowd is devouring the waves with demoralizing consistency, leaving nothing for you to enjoy, Suicides has a secret that you can use to your advantage. Some of the waves peak up on the inside for a nifty little right that most people either aren't aware of, or disdain for the longer lefts. But the waves will punish you for discovering their secret, because with no channel on the rights you will have to battle your way back out for another dose of pleasure.

But it's nothing to feel suicidal over.

OAHU GETS ALL THE BREAKS!

Suicides Mission
A good break for those hungry for non-crowded performance surf. Here's your ticket to adventure:

Short right

Coral shelf

Long wall

75 yards to break

BEWARE! Coral heads

Coral

Paddle out

Paddle out

Showers

Diamond Head Park

Paddle out

Beach

Suicides:
This break is best at 5 feet and under on a Southeast swell and North winds. You can expect hollow sections and long, rippable walls, but watch out for the coral heads and the old pier pilings.

Ricebowl

Location: In front of Outrigger Canoe Club

Activities: Shortboard surfing, longboard surfing, bodyboarding

Wave: Hollow short right and hollow long left

Difficulty: Intermediate and advanced surfers

Prime time: April through September

Wave range: All swells with any south, 4-8 feet, best on southeast or south

Amenities: Parking in Kapiolani Park

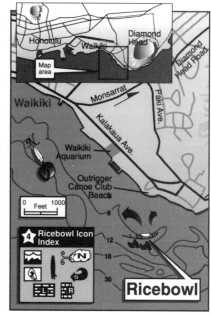

If you are fortunate enough to catch Ricebowl when it is putting on a show, count yourself one of the favored few. For most of the year the reef at Ricebowl slumbers, and is only aroused when seriously juicy summer swells start scrubbing the coral with a whitewater bath. Even when the big swells awaken the reef from its repose and the waves start breaking, it takes a medium tide combined with a south swell and either north winds, light trades or glassy conditions to make Ricebowl perform to its potential.

But when that happens, it is one of life's memorable experiences. The wave leaps up as it hits the shallow reef, and immediately presents the surfer with a dilemma: do you opt for the short but intensely hollow right, or the long and sometimes equally hollow left?

The other surfers in the lineup are usually eager to help resolve that dilemma with their own wave-selection decisions, but each option offers a chance for tubular intimacy with the wave.

On the right, a steep drop is followed by a fast, hollow section that ends in a well-developed channel with an easy paddle back to the lineup.

The left starts out with a deceptively easy section, and builds up momentum as it hits a series of hollow bowls, hence the spot's colorful name. This wave permits a splendid combination of performance surfing and hard-driving tube riding. It's every bit as good as the paralyzingly crowded Ala Moana Bowl, but much more reluctant to display its charms to surfers. It only gets good a handful of times each summer.

Many surfers speak of the power of Town's summer waves with sneering condescension, and for the most part that derision is well deserved. But a wipeout at Ricebowl can wipe that sneer right off your face and stuff it down your throat as the wave delivers a hellish pounding.

These waves have juice, and the inside section on the lefts can slap you off your board and slam you onto the reef before you can squeak in dismay. Just remember as you tuck into that tube or launch into a floater or lip bash, you should have some reasonable expectation of making the maneuver or Ricebowl will make you wish you had never tried.

Although Ricebowl has a devoted group of followers, the crowd here is much less troublesome than at other South Shore spots of equal quality, and your chances of catching your share of waves and having a good time are quite good.

The best place to stash your car is in Kapiolani Park, as near the water fountain or the Natatorium in the Diamond Head end of the park as possible.

If you park near the Natatorium, paddle out through the channel at Sans Souci Beach in front of the New Otani Kaimana Beach Hotel, and paddle toward Diamond Head until you find a knot of surfers clustered just past the Outrigger Canoe Club.

If you park near the Kapiolani Park fountain, continue walking along the road toward Diamond Head until you come upon a beach right-of-way in the middle of some fancy beach houses. There is an elevated concrete beach walk that is a perfect platform from which to check the waves. The surfers directly in front of the steps down to the ocean are surfing Tonggs, which will probably be a mess of churning white water if Ricebowl is good.

Ricebowl is the next spot toward Waikiki from Tonggs, and easy to reach through a channel between the lefts at Tonggs and rights at Ricebowl.

The lucky few members or guests of the Outrigger Canoe Club have a shady place to park, and after their surf session an easy paddle back in to the club, hot showers, clean towels and toiletries, and a marvelous view of the waves as they sip their favorite drinks and discuss their recent exploits in the waves. Definitely a civilized way to surf.

If you think this right at Ricebowl looks tantalizing, the left is three times as long and doubles your pleasure. Photo: Warren Bolster

Publics

Location: Off west end of Kapiolani Park

Activities: Shortboard surfing, longboard surfing, bodyboarding

Wave: Long, workable left, hollow at low tide

Difficulty: Intermediate to advanced surfers

Prime time: April through September

Wave range: All swells with any south, 3-8 feet, best on southeast or south

Amenities: Parking, restrooms, food concessions, showers, interesting bunch of beachgoers

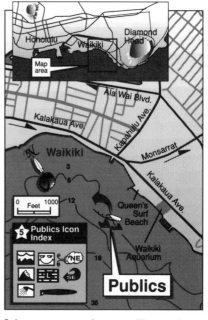

One of the most noticeable and beautiful waves in Waikiki is also one of the most treacherous. From almost any vantage point along Waikiki you can see the waves at Publics peeling as they wind left across the reef with a mantle of wind-blown spray cascading behind. What most people don't notice is the ring of sharp coral that protects this spot from unskilled intruders. When open ocean swells come sweeping in from the south or southeast, they follow the coastline as they wrap around Diamond Head and abruptly hit the shallow reef fronting the Kapiolani Park Beach Center.

This is Publics, site of some of the South Shore's most consistent surf. The configuration of shoreline and the offshore topography act as wave magnets to attract swells, while the deep water of Mamala Bay allows Publics to accommodate large waves. The sight of waves peeling at Publics as seen from almost any other spot in Waikiki has plunged countless surfers into a frustrated frenzy, since whatever spot they are surfing at the moment doesn't seem nearly as consistent or good.

However, the teeth of the guardian reef make this a spot for accomplished wave riders only, and can provide some painfully memorable sessions for beginners and experts alike.

By avoiding the nightmare of surfing Publics at low tide, however, you can slip past the coral heads and save your board and body some trauma. The best route is to walk to the end of the rock groin at the west end of the surf spot, leap into the water and pick your way carefully among the coral heads until you pass the ring of coral and hit deeper water, then head back toward Diamond Head and the lineup.

Another tactic that works on days when the waves are smaller or less consistent is to paddle straight out from the lifeguard station, angling slightly to the left. The water is deeper here, with only a few coral heads right in the impact zone. If your timing is good and you are particularly adept at duck-diving, you can make it out fairly easily.

The best return route to the beach is to paddle over until you are lined up with the lifeguard tower, then catch a wave and force yourself to straighten out, resisting the impulse to shred the wave. By heading straight for the lifeguard tower, you'll stay in the deeper water and avoid the coral heads that lie in wait near the jetty.

If you're not heading for the beach, straightening out on a wave or getting caught inside at the wrong place can be an ordeal, memorable in direct proportion to how much flesh or surfboard fiberglass and foam you leave on the reef. Just keep a cool head and try to maneuver around the coral heads, and carefully pick your places to duck-dive under the waves.

Numerous surfers have been surprised to find that their thruster doesn't work nearly as well as a twin fin after the reef has yanked the third fin off. Other unplanned experiments show that a single-fin board doesn't work well at all when the coral amputates that fin.

As you can imagine, because of the coral heads the crowd at Publics is seldom a factor, and you can usually get enough waves to satisfy yourself in each session.

The winds that blow across the plain of Kaimuki and Kapahulu are usually offshore at Publics and ensure that the waves are usually clean, although southerly winds will blow the waves to pieces.

The tide makes the wave both demonic and heavenly. High tide hides the dangerous coral heads, but makes the long lefts sluggish and somewhat slow. Low tide bares the coral fangs in a snarl, while hustling the waves into a freight train that takes the surfer on a board- and body-challenging speed run, and brings out an occasional tube section.

The park area fronting the surf spot provided Honolulu's citizens at the turn of the century open access to the shoreline, a rarity at that time. The name Publics is the only trace of the Public Baths that served the beachgoing public.

But the waves at Publics are anything but common, and are among Honolulu's best-protected ocean treasures.

Queens

Location: Off Kuhio Beach Park, Waikiki

Activities: Shortboard surfing, longboard surfing, bodyboarding, mat surfing

Wave: Long performance right, slow, mushy left

Difficulty: Beginning to intermediate surfers

Prime time: April through September

Wave range: All swells with any south, 2-5 feet, best on southwest or south.

Amenities: Parking in Kapiolani Park, shower, lifeguard, phones, food concession, equipment rental, attractive beachgoers

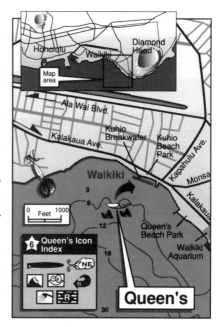

The surf spot Diamond Head from the Waikiki Beach Center at Kuhio Beach Park is an amazing wave factory that produces good surf when most other Honolulu surf spots are waveless. Indeed, it is a rare day that you can't find at least a half-dozen surfers on longboards patiently waiting for a wave that they know eventually will come.

Named Queens Surf after Queen Liliuokalani, who had a home where the beach park is now, the wave itself is well suited for the seemingly conflicting demands of cruising on a longboard and the more frenetic gyrations of shortboard surfing.

With an easy takeoff and steep inside section on the rights, the waves at Queens allow you to effortlessly carve your own surfing statement on their willing walls. The biggest problems are the spot's easy accessibility and popularity, which make for some fairly fierce crowds.

Beginners are easily seduced by the sight of the turquoise waves caressed by an offshore breeze that is funneled around the backside of Diamond Head and across the plains of Kaimuki and Kapahulu and sent straight offshore by the walls of Waikiki's hotels. When malevolent winds come sniffing around Waikiki, Queens always seems to retain nice-looking wave faces while other spots are whipped.

The biggest danger at Queens is the crowd, which is no problem when the experts are out, but can become hazardous in direct proportion to the number of beginners in the lineup. The novice surfer would be better off paddling over to the easier, slower waves next door at Canoes.

The reef at Queens can suck up any limp little swell the ocean is offering and force it to produce a fun wave. But when the serious swells start showing up from Southern Hemisphere storms or nearby hurricanes, Queens is buried under an ocean of white water, and the spot vanishes, only to reappear when the bruiser waves have vanished and the ocean is less threatening.

Queens is that cool, soothing first glimpse of the ocean you see as a reward after you drive through the confusing concrete canyons of Waikiki along Kalakaua Avenue and narrowly miss crashing your car while scrutinizing the amazing display of humanity walking along the sidewalks.

Although the immediate impulse when seeing the waves at Queens is to leap out of your car, sprint across the sand and paddle madly out into the lineup, the nearest parking is at the Honolulu Zoo lot on Kapahulu, or in Kapiolani Park. Although it's a short walk back to Queens, there is the danger that the sight of the crisp, peeling waves will drive you mad before you can grab one for yourself.

The only thing better than watching the tasty waves at Queens is paddling out and giving yourself a royal treat, and then paddling back out for another wave.

Whoever designed the Kuhio breakwater did surfers a great favor by leaving a gap that perfectly frames the break at Queens. The easiest way to get out to the lineup is to paddle across the lagoon, walk across the gap in the breakwater, and then paddle out on the Diamond Head side of the rights. Follow the same path to return to the beach.

With shade, showers, restrooms, food and very intriguing people on the beach, you can turn a session at Queens into a whole day of fun.

If you surf in Waikiki you can expect the occasional Town clown to put you down. But the waves are worth the aggravation. Photo: Warren Bolster

Populars

Location: Offshore of Sheraton Waikiki Hotel

Activities: Shortboard surfing, longboard surfing, bodyboarding

Wave: Long performance right with hollow inside section, short mushy left

Difficulty: Beginner, intermediate, advanced surfers

Prime time: April through September

Wave range: All swells with any south, 4-6 feet, best on southeast or south swell

Amenities: Lifeguard, shower, fascinating crowd on beach, food shops, all within walking distance

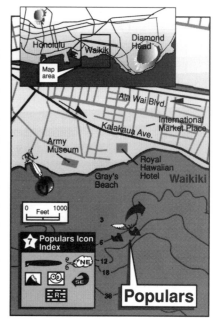

Most surfers seek refuge at Populars, situated between Paradise and Canoes, when the crowd becomes too vicious at other nearby surf spots. But Populars is worth paddling over to simply for the pleasure lurking within its waves. Longboarders love the long walls and easy peaks, while shortboarders crave to carve their initials on Populars' hollow, fast inside section.

When the swell is booming in from the southeast, surfers at nearby breaks can only watch in frustration as Populars fires on all eight cylinders, providing a long wall with exciting sections. A straight south swell will also reward surfers with a good time, while a southwest swell slips past Pops and leaves behind only slight liquid relief to wave-thirsty surfers.

Although it does have its own crew of regulars, Populars is most popular as a haven to mild-mannered surfers frustrated with aggressive crowds at more-famous nearby surf spots. But when the swell lines up with a favorable tide and wind, Populars becomes the main arena, and the hotshots that infest other spots show up in force to take over the break and displace their less aggressive fellow surfers. Still, it's always possible to come away from a session at Pops with a good feeling, knowing you have scored your share of good waves.

When walking up the beach toward Diamond Head from the Fort DeRussy Beach Park, start paddling out when you reach the walkway fronting the Halekulani Hotel. Try to hit the channel between the lefts at Populars and the rights at Paradise, and you'll be in the lineup with no problem.

When approaching from the Royal Hawaiian Hotel, paddle out at the end of the Royal Hawaiian beach and keep to the right of the main break at Populars, and you'll be having fun in the waves before you know it.

Parking is something of a problem here, with the closest lots located in the main parking lot for Fort DeRussy Beach Park, or at Kapiolani Park. The lot at Fort DeRussy is closer to Populars, but civilians aren't allowed to park there before 10 a.m.

You can park anytime you can find a spot at Kapiolani Park, and the longer walk is made much easier by watching the fascinating people cavorting on the beach at Waikiki.

Tennis Courts

Location: Straight out from the tennis courts in Ala Moana Beach Park

Activities: Shortboard surfing, longboard surfing, bodyboarding

Wave: Long performance right with hollow sections, short left

Difficulty: Intermediate and advanced surfers

Prime time: April through September

Wave range: All swells with any south, 4-8 feet, best on south or southwest

Amenities: Parking, lifeguards, phones, shade, food concession

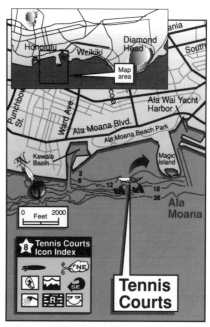

So what do you call a surf spot three hundred yards offshore from some city tennis courts? Tennis Courts, of course. But the game at this splendid Honolulu surf spot is played with surfboards on a liquid court.

Although it can be a real battle for a parking spot in this wildly popular park in the summertime, especially on weekends, holidays and after 10 a.m. any day, persevere and you'll find a good spot.

There are many ways to get out to the pleasure zone at Courts, but two are better than most.

The first is to stand on the beach in front of the tennis courts and gaze seaward past the inner lagoon until you locate three rocks in formation like a family of muskrats trudging through the water. Paddle across the lagoon and to the right of the rocks, and you will be in a slight channel that is deep enough to allow you to gingerly paddle out to the lineup while others who don't know this trick are doing a rock dance on the sharp reef. This channel takes you to the right of the break, which is the deepest channel.

The other technique is to leave your car in the Magic Island parking lot on the Diamond Head end of Ala Moana Park and walk to the right side of the breakwater. Pick your way down the rocks and locate the easiest route through the coral to the deeper water beyond, then paddle down the reef in relative safety from rogue set waves.

Although the paddle out to Courts takes you over some shallow coral and involves a painful reef walk at low tide, the wave is extremely safe. If you're alert enough, you can snag a few waves at other spots on the way down to Courts.

While the rights are the main feature at Courts, the lefts can get good on a southeast swell, and provide a relief outlet for the crowd.

When the wind is right and the swell is cranking, the ride at Courts features a steep takeoff and a long, fast inside section perfect for high-performance surfing. Due to an interesting configuration of the reef, the wave leaves you almost straight in from where you took off, which means you have to paddle through other surfers' waves to get back to the lineup.

While this provides you with a front-row perspective for some hot surfing action, it also makes you a moving impediment, and is definitely not for the fainthearted.

Although it closes out when 8-foot swells start bashing the South Shore, Courts can provide thrills when other spots in Ala Moana Park are too small, or are blown away by a sizable swell.

While it does have a serious crew of regulars, the crowd at Courts is usually mellow enough to allow visitors a few fun waves. Unless, of course, adverse conditions shut down Honolulu's other surf spots, making Courts the only game in town.

Regular-foot surfers weary of the more famous lefts at Kewalos can pounce on the right for a change of pace. Photo: Warren Bolster

Kewalos

Location: Left side of the Kewalo Basin channel
Activities: Shortboard surfing, longboard surfing, bodyboarding
Wave: Long, hollow left; short, fast hollow right
Difficulty: Intermediate and advanced surfers
Prime time: April through September
Wave range: All swells with any south, 3-7 feet, best on south or southeast
Amenities: Parking, showers, restrooms

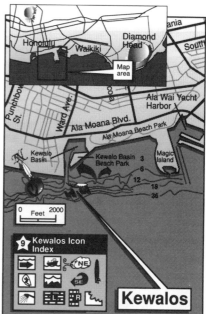

The surfers of Kewalos are as rugged as their surf spot. A working-class wave, it has some nightmarish features to dissuade the weak-willed.

While parking is free, both on the makai edge of Kewalo Basin and across the channel in the state park fronting Point Panic, your car and possessions are vulnerable to theft, which occurs with distressing frequency.

Getting to the surf requires a paddle across shallow, sharp coral, or a trip across the Kewalo Channel, dodging charter and fishing boats. The channel itself is a menacing, rip-current-ravaged forbidden zone that is turned into a churning river of chum as fishing boats jettison their catch cleanings.

The reef is situated so as to attract waves on just about any swell, and will usually have a ridable wave while other nearby spots are starved for surf.

The wave at Kewalos is in character with the harsh surrounding conditions. While on smaller days there is a short, fun right, everyone is really there for the left. It's a full-on, down-the-line screamer that usually is good for a tube when it doesn't spitefully close out and break on your head.

The peak also shifts around, making it difficult to keep a constant position in the lineup. While the first wave in a set might peel perfectly, the next few waves can close out or section prematurely.

And then there are the coral heads that lurk on the inside section edging the channel, waiting to feast on surfboard foam and surfer flesh.

The boat traffic frequently distorts the waves with a cross chop, forcing the walls to do the hula. And the area has a reputation for being sharky, as those predators are attracted by the effluvium from the fishing operations.

But the rough customers who claim Kewalos as their own take pride in surfing such a dangerous spot, and wouldn't trade it for anything.

The state has just improved the whole waterfront area of Kewalo Basin with paved parking, showers, restrooms, landscaping and picnic grounds, smoothing out some of the rough charm of the area and giving the mistaken impression that the surf at Kewalos is civilized. Although the land has been manicured, the waves can be ridden but never tamed.

OAHU GETS ALL THE BREAKS!

West Side Story

Here's four West Shore surf break locations. But take heed oh venturous souls, woe unto you who dare to disrespect local dominion.

Kaena Point

Lighthouse

Dillingham Airfield

Kaena Point Satellite Tracking Station

13

Kaena Point State Park

Makua Valley Rd.

Farrington Hwy.

Waianae Mountain Range

Oahu

Map area

Kili Dr.

12

Makaha Beach Park

Makaha Valley Rd.

Mauna Beach

Waianae Valley Rd.

PACIFIC OCEAN

Mailiilii Channel

Maili Stream

Paakea Rd.

11

Maili Point

Hakimo Rd.

Nanakuli Ave.

10

Hawaiian Electric Beach Park

Hawaiian Electric Company Kahe Power Plant

0 Miles 2

★ Spotlighted breaks

••••• Unsafe Road

— Major roadways

— Subordinate streets

Tracks

Location: North of Kahe Power Plant
Activities: Shortboard surfing, longboard surfing, bodyboarding
Wave: Performance peaks, sometimes hollow, close to shore
Difficulty: Beginner to intermediate surfers
Prime time: Best September through April, breaks all year
Wave range: Southwest, west, northwest swells, 2-6 feet, west is best
Amenities: Parking, shower, great close-up view of surf action

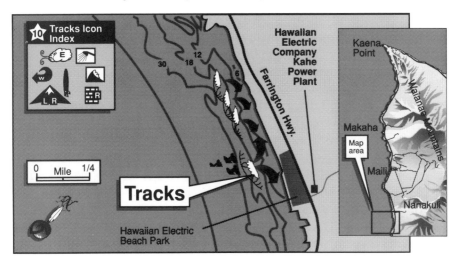

As you head up the Leeward Coast searching for waves, your first sight of the ocean as Farrington Highway finally curves back toward the sea will probably send you scrambling for your surfboard and racing across the abandoned railroad tracks to get to the waves.

The main pleasure pit at Tracks is a reef that offers a long left and short but hollow right. Unfortunately, this is an irresistible lure that attracts the largest, most aggressive crowd, which snatches the prime waves, leaving outsiders to squabble over the scraps.

But unless a miracle occurs and the main reef is temporarily unguarded by the crowd, there is no reason to subject yourself to the stresses of life in the battle zone. Stretching up the coast toward Nanakuli is a series of sandbar and reef breaks that offer short but pulse-pounding rides.

These waves have a dual personality that can satisfy almost the entire spectrum of surfers, except perhaps the hard-core big wave riders. With an offshore wind, medium tide and northwest swell, the rights become full-on hollow grinders that elicit a scream when you make it, and leave you picking sand out of your teeth when you get slammed.

When conditions are less than perfect, the waves become less hollow and much less demanding, offering surfers a chance to dig deeper into their bag of tricks.

Location is everything in surfing just as it is in real estate sales, and Tracks is supremely situated. With its position on the Leeward Coast it can scoop up a variety of northwest, west and southwest swells, making it a year-round fun factory.

When winter's endless stream of serious swells pounds the Leeward Coast, Tracks is the last in a long line of spots to get waves. The same swell that makes Makaha perform at 15 to 20 feet and blows away the area's other surf spots is frequently manageable by the time it arrives at Tracks. The now-tamed swell offers you an alternative to paddling out at giant Makaha and finding out you really don't enjoy life-and-death surfing.

When summer comes around and the northwest and west swells head off for hibernation, the southwest swells stretch, yawn and prod the reef into producing some long lefts, a welcome change from winter's abundance of rights.

Another attractive feature is the fact that the trade winds blow offshore here, and since they are the predominant wind pattern, Tracks is usually keen and clean. It takes a really ill wind from the north or west to make Tracks unridable.

For those surfers weary of the arm-numbing paddle offshore to most of Hawaii's surf spots, Tracks breaks gratifyingly close to the beach. Not only does this make getting in and out easy, but it gives Tracks status as a supreme

Hawaii's waves are so beautiful that they beguile you into forgetting you can be in trouble in waist-deep water. Photo: Dennis Oda

hangout spot. Surfers and their loved ones and friends can enjoy watching the action from the comfort of their cars, as the wave puts the riders almost in their laps.

After years of wrangling, the Nanakuli Surf Club, Hawaiian Electric Co. and the City and County of Honolulu have agreed on a plan to build showers, restrooms and a parking lot on the north end of the beach, a move that would solidify Tracks' position as the Leeward Coast's prime place to watch waves.

When you pass the ominous presence of the Kahe Point Power Plant, your eyes will automatically be riveted by the sight of the ocean, and surfers riding waves. The access to the parking lot is through a deadly break in the Farrington Highway median, site of many fatal accidents.

Tracks gets its name from the railroad tracks still visible near the parking area, which were for sugarcane trains that also served as the main transportation from the Leeward side to Honolulu in plantation days. The name can be stretched with literary license to describe the freight train waves that steam through the area when conditions are right.

Maili Point

Location: On the border between Nanakuli and Maili
Activities: Shortboard surfing, longboard surfing, bodyboarding
Wave: Fast, powerful lefts; some easy peaks
Difficulty: Beginner, intermediate, expert
Prime time: Breaks all year
Wave range: All swells with any west, 3-10 feet
Amenities: Beachfront parking, good view of waves

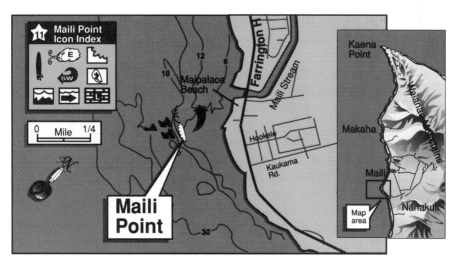

There are a handful of surf spots that possess a menacing aura that makes them seem as though they exist only to test a surfer's resolve. Although Maili Point often dons a benign disguise and allows surfers to have fun sessions, the threatening undercurrent is always present. And when a major swell comes powering through the lineup, Maili Point becomes a proving ground, an arena that breaks some surfers and brings out the beast in others.

Because of its prominent position on the Waianae Coast, the point picks up a satisfying variety of swells. Some surfers swear allegiance to the long lefts that the southwest summer swells deliver, while others defend the honor of the wild waves that come ashore during winter's west and northwest swells.

The end result is a lot of smiles for the Leeward surf legions, who are treated to year-round wave action. The trade winds blow offshore here, and when they are absent the early morning glassy conditions are a refreshing change. However, north winds and kona (west) breezes lacerate the waves and send Leeward Coast surfers elsewhere on search-and-destroy missions.

Maili Point suffers from a personality disorder that makes it take on many appearances, and provides gratification to surfers of wildly divergent abilities. The main point is a bone-crushing left peak that features a steep takeoff followed by quick hollow sections that demand your complete attention and best performance if you wish to escape a memorable beating.

To make it more interesting, the waves shift all over the place, and break erratically. A strong current whips through the lineup and can drag the unwary surfer on a quick trip to the impact zone. The coral shelf here is shallow and merciless, and is punishing both at low and high tide.

On a smaller, clean day Maili Point will smile and show you a good time with long, workable walls and fine tube sections. Come back again, and Maili Point will snarl and slap you around with big sets appearing from nowhere to send you paddling for your life. It's the kind of place where you paddle out thinking you are bad, and the waves show you that you are terrible. But the best way to find out what kind of day it's going to be is to paddle out and give it a go. Those surfers who are looking for a less-stressful surf session will find a good time playing in the peaks across the channel north toward Maili town.

Because of its year-round productivity, Maili Point usually attracts a crowd. However, the punishing waves usually deplete the ranks of surfers in the lineup, and your own ability will determine whether you get any waves.

If you absolutely must leave any valuables in your car, make sure they are hidden, as the parking lot gets worked over pretty well.

The paddle out is rugged, with no real safe area from which to launch. The best trick is to watch where the local surfers enter, and follow them. Failing that, just edge your way across the slippery coral shelf that lines the beach and leap into the ocean when a wave puts a little extra cushion between you and the coral. There is a deep lagoon that leads to the channel between Maili Point and the easy peaks to the right.

Follow the channel out to the lineup, and keep alert for sneaker sets. Although the waves break on a shallow reef shelf, it is fairly narrow and the deeper lagoon is a safe haven when caught inside.

The waves will probably determine how you get to the beach, but your choice will be between heading for the shallow reef shelf in front of the parking lot, or the shallow submerged reef to the Maili side of the river mouth. They are equally treacherous, and caution will spare you a painful encounter.

Despite all the vigorous drubbings the waves at Maili Point have handed out over the years, it is a very popular spot. It is a rare day that good waves aren't immediately pounced upon by area residents and foraging wave snatchers from afar.

But even on those miraculous occasions when you paddle out into some empty waves here, you'll have a feeling tugging at your subconscious that you aren't alone. You probably aren't. Sharks are a noticeable part of the ecosystem at Maili Point, and the fact that the waves break fairly far from shore just adds another bit of texture to an already rough surf spot.

When you're the first person out at dawn or the last person out in the evening, you probably won't be comforted by the fact that most sharks in Hawaii aren't interested in molesting humans.

Makaha

Location: Kaena Point side of Makaha Beach Park
Activities: Shortboard surfing, longboard surfing, bodyboarding, bodysurfing, wave skiing, canoe surfing
Wave: Long performance right, small lefts
Difficulty: Beginners to experts
Prime time: Best September through April, breaks all year
Wave range: All swells with any west, 2-30 feet, west-northwest is best
Amenities: Beachfront parking, great beach, shower, restroom, impromptu parties, beautiful sunsets

Makaha is as close to being the complete ocean playground as is possible on Earth. There is everything here for just about anybody, which is amazing considering how divergent most surfers' tastes are. If you pick four surfers at random, stuff them into a Volkswagen bug and turn them loose on a North Shore surf patrol, hours later they will still be quarrelling over where to surf.

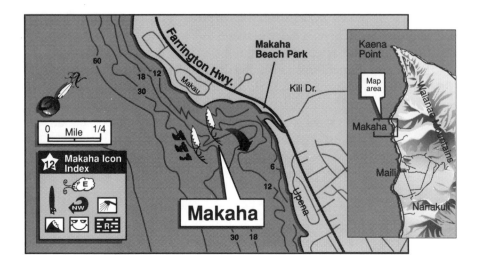

But at one time or another, Makaha satisfies everyone. On the fun days, children and beginners can frolic in the waves close to shore while the hotdoggers shred the waves farther out.

As the waves become a bit more serious, tanker captains can pilot their large craft on the performance waves in the middle of the bay and cruise to the beach in comfort, while rocket riders can fire up their afterburners and challenge the fast, hollow rights that come howling around the point over a shallow reef. As an added bonus, on many days there is a fun left off the backside of the middle peak.

With each increase in wave size, the good-time surfers drop by the wayside and watch from the beach, until only the extremely serious watermen are left.

Makaha is credited with having the largest consistently ridden surf in Hawaii, and even rugged big-wave veterans contemplate with trepidation paddling out on a 25-foot day.

As the waves get bigger, the lineup moves farther and farther out to sea until the safe, sandy shoreline fades from sight. A wipeout and snapped cord out here is the most serious moment you will ever experience in surfing.

Big-wave pioneer Rick Grigg was heading back to the lineup on one such day when he saw Keone Downing plug into a hellacious tube on a frighteningly large wave, and remarked that the lip was so thick that if Keone hadn't done everything just perfectly, he would have died upon impact.

Unlike Waimea Bay, Makaha is much more than a drop when it's big. Once you force yourself over the precipice, you look down the line at a distressingly long wall that frequently ends in a devilish bowl. This is the moment when eternal questions come unbidden to mind, such as Will I die?

Is this worth it? Why did I ever learn to surf? and How quickly can I paddle back out and get another one of these?

If you're not the type that enjoys answering such questions, you'll be pleased to learn that Makaha is fun or merely thrilling more often than it is terminally challenging. This is one of all-too-few places that still maintain a sense of Polynesian hospitality and a feeling of historical perspective. Since ancient times Makaha has been a favored site to test one's surfing ability, and legends have been lived here. The sense of community is still pervasive, and Makaha is a prime place for friends to kick back, sing songs, talk story and hang out.

A typically fun day allows a surfer to carve a delightfully demented path on rippable waves from the middle of the bay to the beach. The truly agile can anticipate the famous Makaha backwash and use it as a launching pad to get some serious air.

Getting in and out is no problem, as the beach is wide and sandy, and the channel is deep and wide. Just remember that the locals will be more impressed by the smile on your face than by any radical surfing you might lay on them.

The crowd is intimidating because from the youngest beach rat to the oldest master, they all have Makaha totally wired. Since the crew here surfs together so often, maximum use is made of every swell, and a wave that escapes to the beach unridden is a cause for astonishment.

Makaha breaks all year, and its position on the Leeward Coast means the trade winds blow offshore. Glassy mornings and evenings are a special treat during winter when the trades break down, and it takes a kona storm or approaching cold front to kick up the westerly winds that make the waves at Makaha ugly.

It's worth the drive to sample the delights of Makaha, and if you stumble onto one of those woolly mammoth swells that convince you to stay on the beach, you're likely to see one of the greatest shows on Earth.

Yokohama

Location: South end, Kaena Point State Park
Activities: Shortboard surfing
Wave: Fast, hollow left, short, mean right
Difficulty: Experts only
Prime time: Best April through September, breaks all year
Wave range: Southwest, west, northwest swells, 4-10 feet, southwest is best
Amenities: Parking, showers, restrooms, close-up surfing action

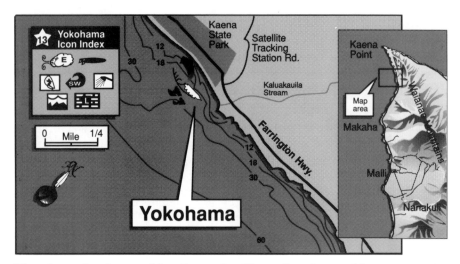

Yokohama

If you're seriously searching for surf and have found something wrong with every surf spot along the Leeward Coast, keep driving until you hit the end of the road.

When the lefts are working, Yokohama is a dramatically beautiful sight certain to start any surfer's glands pumping double-time. Be warned, however, that Yokohama deals out pain in generous doses. If you're not a totally committed surfer in the prime of your ability, you might have a better time enjoying the waves vicariously from the beach. The wave at Yokohama usually starts the day snarling in a bad mood, and is happiest when bashing surfers.

When summer's south swells start booming, savvy west-side surfers smile and start driving north. They know the waves will hit the shallow reef at the south end of Kaena Point State Park and pitch out, forming one of the most exciting and unforgiving waves on the Waianae Coast.

Although the lefts are Yokohama's main attraction, the reef produces a brief but intense right that is cursed with a hammering paddle back out to the lineup.

Summertime is prime time for Yokohama, as the south and southwest swells wrap into the bay and hit the reef at a perfect angle to peel into the channel.

The tide is everything here, though. At high tide the shallow reef floods, leaving the waves somewhat mushy and riddled by the backwash from the beach. Low tide is better, as it lets the wave peak out in deeper water and then slam into the barely moist reef in a hollow howl of protest. But medium tide is best, providing a thrill a minute as the waves hit the shallow reef and leap into the air in surprise, leaving any surfer aboard to free-fall through space.

If surfer and board reach the bottom together, it's time to set a rail for a quick trip into the tube and a quick exit if the tube monster is feeling generous.

Otherwise the wave will deliver a full-body slam onto the reef and a spin-cycle washing machine swirl. If you have cat-quick agility and a supreme belief in your surfing ability, you are in for the time of your life. A bit of sluggishness or a hint of hesitation will earn you a very long and draining day where you can only hope that once the waves are through trouncing you they will wash you up on the beach still clinging to some small shred of dignity.

During winter the swells change direction and come blasting in from the west and northwest, frequently sending the lefts to an oblivion of churning whitewater but opening up the rights a bit. Still, it's worth a winter check just in case the swell is still letting the lefts perform to their full potential.

This is a splendid place for an all-day adventure, with beautiful views of the Waianae Mountains and a wonderfully isolated beach. Yokohama is miles from anywhere, so stock up on provisions in Makaha before you head out.

The surfing action takes place so close to the parking area you're almost tempted to shout advice to the riders. The wave breaks in front of a white sandy beach, and the paddle out to the lefts is easy, helped by a generous and deep channel.

Despite its isolated location and nasty reputation for passing out punishment, Yokohama has devoted followers, a vigilant group of talented Leeward Coast surfers who are joined by the hottest surfers on the island when the word of a good swell gets out.

But if you find most of the other waves along the Leeward Coast too tame and you really want to push your performance level, Yokohama is worth the effort. If you find you'd rather enjoy the show from a safer perspective, you'll not find anyplace with better action.

Yokohama is named after a Japanese sugarcane worker who used to fish in the area in plantation days, and people gradually began calling the area Yokohama, a tradition that continues.

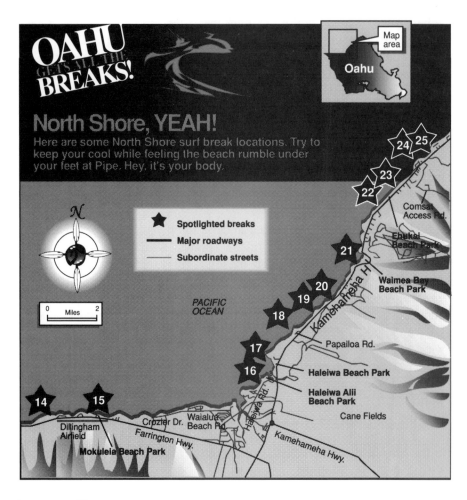

Army Beach

Location: Farrington Highway across from Dillingham Airfield
Activities: Shortboard surfing
Wave: Quick, hollow left
Difficulty: Intermediate, expert surfers only
Prime time: September through April
Wave range: Northwest, west-north-west swells, 5-8 feet
Amenities: Beachfront parking, showers, no crowds

The military has taken away the lifeguards and beach bathrooms at Army Beach in Mokuleia, but the fun zone is fully operational offshore.

As you leave Waialua and cruise Farrington Highway toward Kaena

Point, you are confronted with a bewildering coastline, where unheralded waves break seemingly at random on unfamiliar reefs.

This is the prime habitat for surfers hoping to avoid Oahu's greatest problem: ravening hordes of wave-hungry surfers. If you follow the road long enough it will take you to a little hole in the reef fronting Army Beach. The crease in the reef doesn't seem big enough to shelter a tiny reef fish, let alone offer a surfer haven from surly waves. But when a 6-foot swell combines with a good wind and medium-high tide, the channel is just big enough to make the waves break wonderfully.

Unfortunately, this is a very temperamental surf spot. The wind is usually a wave-lacerating onshore breeze, and only southwest or west winds or glassy conditions can perform the plastic surgery necessary to make the wave faces pretty.

Also, the swell has to be just right or the waves will throw a temper tantrum and pout. Northwest or west-northwest are best, as north and northeast swells slam into the reef sideways and make each takeoff as hopeless as betting on good surf when you have a week free from school or work.

A big swell can cover the puny channel in a frothing sea of white water, and even when the waves are smaller, passing through the channel is as nerve-wracking as walking across a glass-strewn parking lot barefoot and blindfolded.

At low tide the normally exciting trip from the beach through the channel and into the waves becomes a test of nerves, as coral heads bubble up on each side of the channel while the waves and current push you toward the waiting talons.

But boldness is rewarded once you pass the coral gauntlet and reach the lineup. The view from the lineup is exotic, and with no visible evidence ashore of mankind's presence you can trick yourself into believing you are on a Third World surf adventure minus the threats of disease and drudgery.

But the best treat is that charging down from Kaena Point are some of the most savory little saltwater snacks on the island.

The takeoff is an adventure in free flight, as the steep peak frequently causes rider and board to part company. If you make the drop with some composure, the rest of the wave is a rapid blur of fast sections and gaping caverns, perfect for getting to know these waves from the inside out. If you can't find your way into and out of these tubes, the wall is perfect for slamming off the lip and launching into whitewater bounces.

The rights are good for a quick peak and a savage beating on the paddle back out, but the lefts are so fine and so frequently uncrowded that most surfers don't bother, unless they need the paddling practice.

Because of the foreboding presence of the shallow reef and the fact that most surfers can satisfy their wave lust without driving so far, many sessions at Army Beach are shared with only a few friends. But as each year the crowds continue to escalate beyond belief, surfers are being pushed to the fringe areas and solo sessions are becoming relegated to the realm of dreams and memories.

Until the dreary day arrives that all of Mokuleia is covered in housing and resort developments, this is still adventureland. The drive to Army Beach is made delightful by the open cane fields, the brooding green presence of the Waianae Mountains, and glimpses of empty reefs where waves break unmolested.

The parking lot at Army Beach provides a front-row view of the waves, and the beach is white and warm. To locate the channel and safe passage into the lineup, study the waves a bit and notice where the waves finally peter out in a tired little foam ball. This is your saltwater ski lift, and if you paddle quickly and time the sets well, you'll be in the lineup in moments.

Getting back to the beach is a snap; just ride a wave until it quietly expires, then scratch like mad for the channel and the beach. If you haven't overstayed your welcome into the low-tide misery zone, you'll quickly be showering off and searching for food. Otherwise, the coral will probably exact its toll of flesh and you'll be clutching a battered board with bloody fingers and wondering what went wrong.

But leaving a little blood on the reef isn't much of a price to pay for a day of great waves, shared only by a few friends.

Mokuleia Beach Park

Location: Farrington Highway past Waialua
Activities: Shortboard surfing, sail-boarding
Wave: Fast performance right, often hollow
Difficulty: Intermediate and expert surfers
Prime time: September through April
Wave range: Northwest, north, northeast swells, 3-8 feet
Amenities: Oceanfront parking, showers, camping, restrooms

There is a place on the North Shore where you can pull up in your car to check the waves, shower off after a surf session and use a real bathroom to answer nature's call.

It is seldom crowded, and features riveting, high-performance waves. Sounds like another surf fantasy, right? Well it is, but at times this fantasy becomes reality.

Except for maddeningly rare glassy mornings and west-wind days, Mokuleia Beach Park is cursed by a sideshore breeze that is the delight of windsurfers but leaves the waves too afflicted with the mumps to make surfers happy.

Another vigilant guardian that keeps the crowds at bay is a vigorous, sharp and shallow reef that is certain to capture your attention except at high tide.

Further, the beach park waves close out on most swells over 8 feet, which happens pretty often during the winter surf season, and the reef is very particular about which swell directions will permit the waves to break correctly.

But when it's on, this fickle surf spot delivers a dose of undiluted surf serum. This screeching right wall is a full-speed run that tests your board's ability to fly, and your ability to stick with your board as it zips from section to section.

The ever-present reef also tests your nerve, and a full commitment to making the wave is necessary to keep you from painfully merging your body parts with the coral.

If you don't mind the risk of bouncing off the reef as a penalty for failure to fly, the beach park's hollow sections will tempt you to toss caution aside for a memorable glimpse into the waves' innards.

There are two peaks at work here, with the outside peak handling the bigger waves and offering a steep takeoff and a somewhat slack section that you can toy with by dipping into your bag of tricks. If you spend too much time fooling around on the first peak, you'll be dead in the water right when you need a burst of speed to slingshot you into the hollow section. You will need that momentum to plug into the barrels with some reasonable hope of exiting, as the only thing that works on this section is rail-to-rail speed lines.

Getting out to the waves here is less difficult than climbing a cliff with your feet bound together, but not much. The beach is rocky, and a slippery ledge of coral lines the immediate offshore area. The best tactic to reach the waves is to slowly sure-foot it over the ledge until you reach deeper water on the very inside edge of where the waves break, then paddle around the end section, taking care to miss the coral heads loitering to grab chunks out of your board.

Once you make it beyond the break, shift into a foraging mode to pounce on any empty waves that might try to slip by as you paddle out to the main peak.

After the inevitable wipeout, your options for getting back to the lineup are limited. You can take your chances and paddle like mad straight back out, hoping a set doesn't swoop down and punish you for such impudence. Luckily, the outside peak and the shallow inside section are separated by an area of deeper water, so if you head for that slack zone you just might escape back to the lineup with little trouble.

A safer tactic is to take the long stroke over to the channel past the inside section. As the surf gets bigger, the last option becomes more appealing.

Unfortunately, everything has to come together to make the waves work well at the beach park. You can waste a lot of time and gas searching for a good time here, and spend many despondent moments sitting on the park grass watching waves being mauled by a malevolent wind.

But when it's on, you won't find a finer spot on the island for taking your board on a fiberglass-searing speed mission. And when the sets slack off enough to give you time to contemplate the mysteries of life, you just might be treated to the sight of gliders drifting along on an updraft, or parachutists floating gently to earth on a tropical breeze, both from the Dillingham Air Field across the street. If the winds are blowing wrong, you might even have a chance to rescue an errant jumper from the waves.

Haleiwa

Location: Off Haleiwa Alii Beach Park
Activities: Shortboard surfing, long-board surfing, bodyboarding
Wave: Fast performance right, often hollow; shorter left
Difficulty: Beginner through expert
Prime time: September through April
Wave range: West-northwest, north-west swells, 2-12 feet
Amenities: Parking, showers, restrooms, lifeguard, beach center

Haleiwa can be a dream come true or your worst nightmare. If you are alert, sometimes you can tell what kind of day it's going to be while watching the waves from the beach and possibly save yourself a brutal beating.

Unfortunately, Haleiwa frequently dons a delectable disguise that makes the waves appear alluring, at least while you are warm and dry on the sand. But once you paddle out for a closer glimpse and the waves have you in their clutches, Haleiwa drops its disguise and delivers a drubbing that will make you rue the day you caught your first wave.

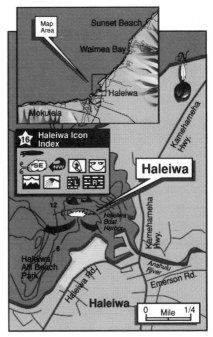

Getting out at Haleiwa is the first obstacle, as you have to time the sets perfectly before you paddle out over the shallow inside section affectionately dubbed the toilet bowl. No matter how exquisite your timing, a set always seems to materialize at the worst possible moment, dashing you on the coral.

Once you are in the lineup, the current is a relentless river that will drag you off to Waimea Bay if you rest for the briefest of moments. On a bad day you can spend your entire surf session struggling against the rip. Some surfers prepare for a contest by paddling out at Haleiwa on a horrendous day just to battle the rip and sharpen their paddling skills.

But the absolute worst aspect of a Haleiwa surf misadventure is the focusing area, which causes 5-foot waves and 8-foot waves to break 100 yards apart. If you surf Haleiwa, you will soon be prodded to find out how quickly you can paddle that far.

If you sit far enough out to catch the bigger waves, you'll miss all the insiders. And if you sit outside long enough you'll begin to envy the surfers having such a good time on the inside and paddle into join them just in time to be pummeled by a set of no escape and dragged backward to the beach.

But there's more. When you finally catch your sweet reward and are taking out your frustrations on the wave, you'll be paying a return visit to the toilet bowl, which waits patiently for a chance to end your wave with a fin-snapping, body-scraping closeout section.

The problems just get bigger as the waves increase in size, until on a solid 8-foot day with rogue 12-foot sets you will spend your whole time paddling against the rip and still be too far over and out to catch anything. Then a set will loom on the horizon and send you stroking madly. The waves will cruelly raise your hopes by letting you escape the first wave, only to thump you with the rest of the set.

It is unavoidable that you will get caught inside at Haleiwa. You can spend the day hovering timidly 20 yards farther out than anyone, bolting at the first sign of a set, and you'll still get nailed by a maverick wave. Once you realize the inevitability of this, you can relax and enjoy your surf session secure in the knowledge that nothing you do will help and you might as well have some fun anyway.

Ah, but then there are the good days, when a northwest swell is caressed by an easterly wind on a medium tide, and everybody else resisted the urge for a dawn patrol. That's what keeps people coming back for more, despite repeated beatings at Haleiwa. This wave has juice to spare, and even a 5-foot day with bigger sets will provide thrills and chills, workable walls and hollow sections, and a wonderfully steep drop on takeoff.

Because it breaks on a wide variety of swells, the full spectrum of surfers can have fun here. Little grommets can frolic in safety near shore on the reform section while on the outside reef the serious surfers are working-over the powerful peaks.

The park is a prime spot for checking the waves to determine the wisdom of paddling out, as well as admiring the rides of the legion of hot surfers who are slaves to Haleiwa's charm whether it's 5 feet or maxing out.

The absolute best route to the lineup seems suicidal, as it entails taking the toilet bowl head on. Starting from the far left corner of the beach, paddle slowly toward the toilet bowl and linger until a big set breaks. When the last of the white water is boiling over the shallow reef, start stroking straight out. Take care not to veer to the right where the other surfers are sitting, or the rip will carry you past your objective.

Some people so dread the toilet bowl that they delude themselves into thinking that a paddle out around the lefts is a clever plan. It's not. Not only will the waves push you out into Haleiwa Harbor, once you make it into deeper water the rip will force you to fight for every inch as you struggle to reach the lineup.

There are some demented individuals who actually thrive on the adverse conditions at Haleiwa, and excel in the waves while others around them are being battered. These people can take care of themselves, but almost everyone else is comforted by the presence of the lifeguards, who get a vigorous workout each winter saving surfers who have an inflated estimation of their ability.

A quick chat with the lifeguards before you paddle out might make sure that you don't meet the guards under more serious and embarrassing circumstances.

Puaena Point

Location: East end of Haleiwa Beach Park
Activities: Shortboard surfing
Wave: Fast, hollow right, sporadic lefts
Difficulty: Intermediate to expert surfers
Prime time: September through April
Wave range: West-northwest, northwest, north swells, 3-12 feet, northwest is best
Amenities: Parking, camping, showers, restrooms

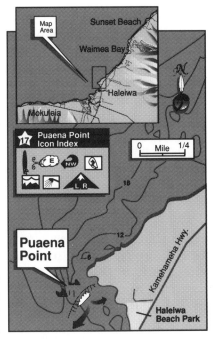

When a rising swell assaults the North Shore and the surf spots begin to be overwhelmed one by one, surfers start choosing their favorite alternatives. Some grab their big-wave boards and head for Waimea Bay, where movie and still cameras will record their every triumph and trauma. A very few others seek the anonymity of the outer reefs, either taking a boat or making the long, lonely paddle, and far from shore confront the demon within themselves. Some head for Makaha and other spots on the Leeward or Windward sides of the island, where the swell becomes more manageable as it wraps around the coast. And others seek safety and fun in the little nooks and crannies right in the impact zone on the North Shore. Puaena Point is one such haven of refuge. When the swell rages out of control at other spots, Puaena comes alive.

Although it juts into the open ocean at the northeast tip of Waialua Bay, the reef points at just the right angle to soothe the savage swell. When the east wind is blowing offshore and the swell is northwest on a medium tide, Puaena offers a quick, hollow right that is a tuberider's delight. On a more westerly swell the left opens up and offers a fun alternative, though it can't match the speed and barrels the right provides in such abundance.

A few elements keep Puaena from being pure perfection. A constant current running through the lineup can drag you off to a desolate stretch of coastline. And, as might be expected of an area so close to a fishing boat harbor, the lurking menace of sharks prowling the lineup keeps surfers entertained during lulls and early morning or late afternoon sessions.

When the swell shifts a bit and starts coming in on a more northerly tack, the far point beckons with seemingly open and makable waves. This is another of the ocean's clever ruses, designed to lure you to your doom. Not only do these waves zip along faster than any surf vehicle ever devised in fevered imaginations, they break over a particularly nasty reef. When you finally are forced from your fantasy back to reality by an unmakable section and you straighten out, the white water will propel you toward a shoreline of jagged limestone rocks. The far point also lacks even the hint of a channel to get you back into the lineup easily, and the sets can drag you right back onto the rocks you so recently avoided.

The far point has been ridden on some distressingly large days by surfers who take great delight in such a challenge, and who are happiest when the conditions are at their absolute worst.

It's all theirs.

Most surfers will be pleased with Puaena proper, which combines a steep, double-suck takeoff with an immediate hollow section for a screaming tube. You would have to be the sorriest surfer who ever lived not to get barreled here, as these waves do everything but ride your board for you to ensure tubular intimacy. Getting back into the lineup is no problem, as the wave tapers off on the inside section and the shallow, flat coral shelf empties quickly into deeper water.

The easiest path to the lineup is to walk around the ironwood-pine-covered point on the right-hand edge of the park and paddle out from the sandy cove. Head for the edge of the waves, and slip through during a lull.

Getting back to the beach is a matter of straightening out in the white water and milking it to shore.

Because the waves at Puaena are so visible from Kamehameha Highway, when it's good it is usually packed. But if you can paddle against the current and maintain a good position lineup, you'll be able to commandeer your share of tubes. The crowd will make sure you don't get more than your share.

Himalayas

Location: Across from Meadow Gold Dairy
Activities: Bodyboarding, shortboard surfing, longboard surfing, big-wave board surfing
Wave: Small fun rights, giant long lefts, sometimes hollow
Difficulty: Intermediate to expert surfers
Prime time: Best September through April
Wave range: West-northwest, northwest, north, northeast, 4-40 feet
Amenities: Unpaved beachfront parking

You will probably never surf this place, and if you do, you will most likely wish you hadn't. Surfers are always eyeing Himalayas speculatively from nearby surf spots, and many have interesting stories about surfing there that usually involve a harrowing session spent scampering to keep from getting pounded.

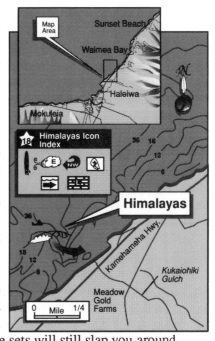

First of all, the waves break a very lonely distance from the beach, and are bounded by a fierce current. The lineup also has a demonic focusing area, which means that 5-foot waves and 10-foot waves during the same swell break hundreds of yards apart, making for some heart-thudding stroking.

If you linger inside hoping to have a little fun on the smaller waves, the sets will slap you around. If you wait out the back for the big mackers, you'll miss all the inside waves and the sets will still slap you around.

On a big day, Himalayas can be as exciting as rolling a car on a hairpin turn, especially if you survive. The sight of an approaching outside set can freeze the marrow in your bones, and when your frantic paddling proves futile, the impact of the waves can suck that frozen marrow right out, leaving you a spineless blob bobbing in the ocean far from shore.

But it isn't always life or death out at Himalayas. When a prime north swell packs nearby Laniakea with rabid surfers snarling at each other, a splendid right and left peak combination shows up at Himalayas.

On 5- to 8-foot west-northwest swells the lefts at Himalayas can be a treat, with long walls and a hollow bowl section. On those same swells a right appears on the back door that offers a frustrating paddle for a wave that jacks up just as you've given up on it, and turns into a steep peak with a quick wall and sporadic hollow sections.

Of course, since there is no channel on the rights, the paddle back out can teach you everything you didn't want to know about your paddling deficiencies.

For the truly crazed, big swells peak up way out in a big, big ocean and provide more blood-chilling excitement than Waimea ever can, and without the crowds of incompetents that make Waimea so dangerous.

On a big day at Himalayas you will be alone, or accompanied only by whomever you can trick into joining you on a journey to the outer limits. There are some deranged souls who are happiest when Himalayas is raging and there is no other human in the water for miles to dilute their adventure.

Fortunately, when Himalayas is breaking, other, better spots are also breaking. It's a fickle wave, needing just the right combination of swell, tide and wind to break well, and surfers aren't enticed very often to challenge these distant, brooding peaks.

Each winter swell brings out a different nuance of Himalayas' character, but the best winds are either dead glass, light easterlies or moderate southeast breezes.

Getting into the lineup here is far easier than it should be, considering the aquatic abuse that awaits the unwary. Just locate the channel between Laniakea and Himalayas, launch into the water and ride the rip seaward until you reach your chosen peak. This channel is big and deep and only closes out on the inside under dire circumstances.

On the perfect day, with the perfect swell and perfect wind, you just might end up snagging the wickedest, longest peeling left of your life.

But while contemplating whether to paddle out here, it might be well to reflect that the spot was named when someone compared wiping out here to taking a tumble in the Himalaya Mountains.

Jocko's

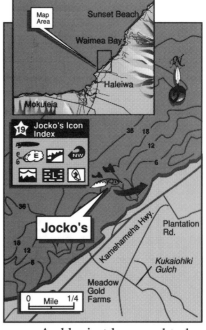

Location: Across the channel from Chun's Reef
Activities: Shortboard surfing
Wave: Fast, steep left, frequently hollow
Difficulty: Intermediate and expert surfers
Prime time: September through April
Wave range: West-northwest, northwest swells, 4-10 feet
Amenities: Limited beachfront parking, shower within walking distance

Consider the luck of Jock Sutherland, who grew up in a house with a prime view of a splendid left-breaking wave. And he just happened to be a goofyfoot.

Unfortunately, before leashes were invented, Jock couldn't convince many people to join him for a session. The wave in front of his house broke on some nasty coral heads, and Jock's friends became unhappy when the rock-lined shore exploited their wipeouts by gobbling up their surfboards.

The prospect of lonely surf sessions didn't daunt Jock, as he is one of the surfing world's most brazen characters and thus spent many dangerous missions with just his thoughts to keep him company as he surfed in his own backyard.

These days solo sessions aren't a problem, as the security of leashes has made bold rogues out of nearly everyone. On a good swell there is usually a small army of surfers eager to plunder the waves at Jocko's.

But the crowds at Jocko's are mere pitiful imitations of the zealous hordes that haunt the North Shore's more famous left at Pipeline. You can still paddle out at Jocko's on a good day with a reasonable hope of getting some great tube rides without being stuffed into the pit by callous crowds.

Which is not to say the waves let you ride with impunity. The rocks are still there, in the water and lining the beach, patiently waiting to devour surfers and surfboards. The waves are still eager as ever to whack surfers and spank them all the way to the beach, a particularly disagreeable prospect when you are being dragged toward flesh-flaying rocks.

An incoming tide is best at Jocko's, as it provides at least the illusion of a watery covering on the rocks. A full high tide will make the waves break farther inside right on top of these board-breaking beasts.

With a rising 6-foot swell and steady east wind or glassy conditions, Jocko's is a pure delight. The sets drifting down from Laniakea jack up and start to zip down the line toward the bowl. If your paddling is proficient and your timing is superb, you can snag one of these sidewinders for a quick free-fall, then turn into an immediate tube, followed by a quick recovery section and a return match with the tube monster as you hit the bowl.

These waves will put a smile on your face even if they are being coy about rolling out the barrels, as the walls are perfect for floaters, lip bashes, whitewater bounces and anything else your inspired imagination might dream up.

Some swells feature a good right off the back side of the left peak that is marred only by the lack of even the suggestion of a channel. Each paddle back out on the rights is an adventure, complete with waves that detonate on your head before dragging you screaming to the rock-lined shore.

The lineup for the lefts usually features two distinct peaks, and it's a good idea to decide which peak you desire the most and hang out there. Otherwise you'll end up paddling between peaks all session and end up with exercise instead of good rides.

The first peak is farthest over toward Kaena Point, and attracts the down-the-line, biggest waves at Jocko's. If you can't flog your board into top speed and have to straighten out, you could end up on a runaway ride into the rocks.

The sight of water swirling around rocks that magically appear when you are caught inside will probably inspire your body to unimagined heights of performance. Use this newfound energy to help the current as it carries you toward the channel, and keep paddling parallel to the rocks, toward the channel and slightly out to sea.

The other peak swings wide and jacks up closer to the channel, and is a steep drop followed by the hollow bowl section. If the wave wallops you here, the resulting explosion will blast you past the rocks and toward the channel.

The few parking spots along Kamehameha Highway fill up quickly when there is surf, and it's a miracle that more surfers aren't killed as they divert their attention from the hazards of the highway to gape at the waves.

Getting out to the lineup is simple, as the channel between Jocko's and Chun's is wide and deep. If the channel disappears underneath a river of churning white water, that is a serious clue that the waves are grumpy that day and don't want to be disturbed.

The absolute best way to get to the beach is to ride a wave to the channel and then stroke with conviction against the current. If that doesn't work, you can paddle across to Chun's for a wave to either straighten out on or ride to the beach. The waves will probably decide which option you employ.

With increasing numbers of surfers becoming completely deranged by visions of fame and glory at the sight of all the cameras at Pipeline, more surfers have begun to opt for the more private pleasures of Jocko's. This is where local residents and wily international pros slip away for a less stressful but equally tube-filled session.

However, there still are elements that help guard Jocko's against being saturated by surfers. Being blasted toward the rocks while clinging helplessly to your board or being dragged backward by your leash is a memory that will haunt you for a lifetime.

Chun's Reef

Location: Off Kamehameha Highway between Laniakea and Waimea Bay
Activities: Shortboard surfing, longboard surfing, bodyboarding
Wave: Fun performance right, shorter left
Difficulty: Beginning to expert surfers
Prime time: September through April
Wave range: West-northwest, north-west, north, northeast swells, 2-8 feet, northwest is best
Amenities: Beachfront parking, shower

Tired of being trounced by snarling peaks, ripped by ravenous reefs and menaced by monstrous waves? Do yourself a favor and head for Chun's Reef. If you can't look good while surfing Chun's, it's time to take up another sport.

The biggest danger in surfing the easy, rippable waves at Chun's is tripping over your newly inflated ego. Fortunately, the other surf spots on the North Shore specialize in humbling surfers. When a northwest swell up to 6 feet combines with easterly trade winds to pay a visit to Chun's Reef, the waves are eager to help any surfer believe he is the hottest rider that ever sizzled the seas.

Chun's has it all: a long wall custom-made for multiple lip bashes, floaters or endless nose rides; a hollow section for the occasional tube ride; a nice safe channel for an easy return to the fun zone; and sporadic lefts to lighten the load of the crowded rights.

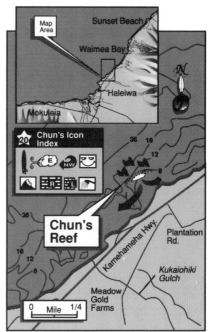

The worst part is that this wave doesn't have the decency to make even a feeble attempt to shield itself from public view, but rather flaunts its delights to anyone driving by on Kamehameha Highway.

With such an ego-gratifying fun wave so easily visible, you can be sure you'll never have to worry about surfing Chun's alone. Every part of every wave is utilized with maximum efficiency, and nothing goes to waste.

On a good day, you will take off on a wave only to have a longboarder stall you out with a fade turn while a bodyboarder drops into your lap and two paddlers taking a shortcut through the lineup stroke frantically in front of you. But there are a few tricks you can employ to ensure that you get your share of solo waves.

Chun's is actually four different peaks that change with each subtle shift in swell direction. The first peak is the bowl, which leaps up on the edge of the channel and is a thrilling takeoff that quickly dissipates, though at times it can wind into the inside hollow section.

The next peak is the middle section, which is where the main crowd hangs out to snag the delicious walls that peel for a hundred yards all the way into the inside section.

Then there are the long shots that jump up 30 yards beyond the middle peak and either offer a speed run to the channel, or close out near the bowl after an exciting ride.

As an added bonus, the middle peak and bowl often feature a left off the backdoor that helps spread out the crowd. While the lefts can offer a fast wall

65

and fun alternative to the packed rights, the paddle back out is hampered by the rest of the set and keeps the lefts from being exploited by very many surfers.

The trick to vacuuming up your quota of waves is to keep a sharp lookout, time the sets and paddle either toward the bowl or the far peak just before each particular set arrives. It takes equal parts cunning, alertness and luck, but if you keep your wits about you the crowd will watch with envy as you always magically seem to be in the right spot for each set.

Chun's will break on a variety of swells, from west-northwest through northeast, but northwest is prime time. It also looks fine on a full spectrum of wind conditions, including early morning and evening glass, most trade winds, and southeast, south, and southwest breezes. But you won't have to even see the waves to know whether they are working, as Kamehameha Highway near Chun's will resemble the world's largest used-car lot of disreputable autos.

Most people sprint straight out through the channel to get to the waves, while a crafty few walk up the beach a hundred yards and paddle toward the lineup, letting the waves and the current shunt them toward the channel, thus saving a few hundred strokes.

The best way back to the beach is to ride a wave until you have drained the absolute last gasp of energy, then paddle away from the parking area up the beach toward the dry river bed. Not only will this keep you from battling the rip in the channel, but it will put you ashore close to the shower, provided by the generosity of Rick Ralston of Crazy Shirts.

There is something sensually delightful about showering off in fresh water after a good session while watching surfers carving up the waves that exhaustion recently forced you to abandon.

About the only people who never admit to surfing Chun's are the serious big-wave warriors, who probably sneak out into the harmless waves for a fun session when no one's looking.

Waimea Bay

Location: Waimea Bay Park
Activities: Shortboard surfing, bodyboarding, bodysurfing, big-wave board surfing
Wave: Giant right point wave, pounding shorebreak
Difficulty: Advanced to expert surfers
Prime time: October through March
Wave range: West-northwest, northwest, north, northeast swells, 6-30 feet, northwest is best
Amenities: Parking, showers, restrooms, lifeguards, picnic area

When winter's biggest waves come wrapping into the bay at Waimea, everyone pauses to admire one of nature's great muscle shows. It's a display of power that people remember forever.

A handful of brave souls challenges that power, and while the number of challengers increases every year, it's still a small, select group that actually rides the waves at Waimea. The rest just head out and get underfoot as they paddle desperately to escape a beating from the waves.

There is no magic aura that protects Waimea from surfing's greatest menace: crowds. At most breaks crowds are a problem. At Waimea they are life-threatening, and make a dangerous situation positively insane.

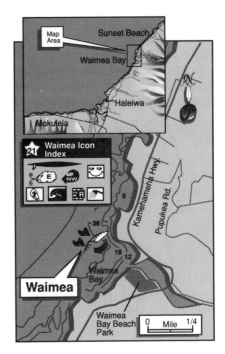

The serious Bay boys reckon there are two kinds of surf at Waimea, fun stuff under 25 feet, and anything bigger, which they deem exciting.

Actually, there is a third type of surf at Waimea. When the swell is too small for the point to break, the waves hug the rocks on the inside at a spot named Pinballs. Although Pinballs in no way resembles the harrowing peak at Waimea Point, it does possess a very juicy takeoff and workable wall. If you're keen to tell your friends back home you surfed Waimea, you can have a fun session at Pinballs and technically qualify as a Bay rider.

The hopelessly hooked Waimea Bay addicts don't even glance at the waves when Pinballs is breaking. They live only for those few times each winter when unimaginably powerful swells come blasting into Waimea. These waves march into the Bay in tight formation, and leap into the air when they hit the reef at the point, providing the most terrifyingly pleasing few seconds in all of surfing.

With traffic on Kamehameha Highway at a stunned standstill, people in stalled cars and those standing and sitting on the beach and surrounding cliffs focus their attention on the knot of surfers clustered near the point. The combined energy of the crowd is almost visible, as people cheer late takeoffs and groan at the terrible wipeouts.

When a surfer is ripped from his board by the wave, he's lucky if the wave doesn't swat him with it. He's also lucky if the rest of the set doesn't drag him so deep his eardrums rupture. And he's very lucky if the waves merely drag him to the beach and dump him on the sand, an exhausted, sodden lump. The unlucky surfer is battered and beaten and given a free tour of the Bay by the current, until lifeguards or the Fire Department's rescue helicopter can pull him out.

When surfing Waimea it is essential to have the proper crazed attitude that implies a certain reckless disregard for personal safety. If you paddle out thinking you are going to get hurt, you will. If you think you can't make the drop, you won't, and if you begin to wonder what in the world you're doing out among those menacing waves it's time to be thankful you're still alive and head for the beach.

But a positive attitude is useless without the physical ability to help you survive a meaningful encounter in the lineup. If your body isn't conditioned by rigorous training to withstand dreadful punishment from giant waves, being dragged rapidly to painful depths and enduring prolonged periods without blessed air, your Waimea experience is likely to be short, nasty and brutish. If you are in excellent physical shape, your Waimea adventure is still likely to be short, nasty and brutish, but your chances of surviving are much better.

Getting into the lineup at Waimea sounds much simpler than the grim reality. Most Waimea vets gather across the river mouth on the right side of the Bay, waiting until the last wave of a set breaks. They then charge the shorebreak and hit the water paddling full blast, pushing through the waves and letting the current carry them to the middle of the Bay.

While the big-wave boards dominate Waimea Point, bodyboarders have carved a spectacular niche for themselves in the punishing waves in the middle of the bay. Be warned: this is for seriously deranged experts only. Photo: Warren Bolster

The trick is to keep away from the white water near the rocks, and yet miss the ligament-wrenching lefts that grind through the middle of the Bay. Then it's a matter of heading for the lineup and finding someone who looks like he's having a good time out there. Attach yourself to him like a remora, and hope he really knows what he's doing and is not just another genial lunatic.

Presuming everything goes well and that you are still in control of your faculties and that your board is in one piece when you decide you have had enough, the route to the beach is simple: ride the white water in as far as you can, and stick close to the rocks. If you drift into the middle of the Bay, the lefts will do their best to test the limits of your limbs by stretching every ligament, tendon and joint seemingly to the breaking point.

If you and your board part company, resist the urge to flail madly toward the beach. Just help the rip carry you on the Bay tour, ducking under the sets when possible, until you can head for the rocks on the point. Then let the white water carry you in. If that seems like too rugged an endeavor, then head for deep water outside the breaking waves and tread water until the rescue helicopter can come scoop you out. While you wait you can try to delude yourself into believing things could always be worse. They could, but not much.

Each year the Bay is visited by groups of people who challenge the neck-wrenching shorebreak. Although it might appear to be less dangerous than an assault on 20-foot waves at the point, the shorebreak has compiled an impressive tally of maimed and drowned bodyboarders and bodysurfers. More people run into trouble 20 yards from shore than farther out in bigger waves at the point.I have always thought that if it was your fate to die while surfing, there would be few superior times and places than at Waimea during a classic 25-foot swell. What better way to go than with hundreds of people watching your final ride, movie and still cameras capturing your ultimate glory, and the comforting presence of rescue helicopters and lifeguards on jet skis just in case it wasn't your time to die?

But if you want to live, it's a good idea to check with the lifeguards and really be honest with yourself as you watch the waves and decide whether your first session out at Waimea might not end up as your last surfing experience.

Banzai Pipeline

Location: Toward Kaena Point from Ehukai Beach Park

Activities: Shortboard surfing, bodyboarding, bodysurfing, big-wave board surfing

Wave: Ultimate hollow left tube, grinding right tube

Difficulty: Intermediate to expert surfers

Prime time: September through April

Wave range: West-northwest, northwest, north-northwest swells, 4-15 feet, northwest is best

Amenities: Parking, lifeguard, showers, restrooms

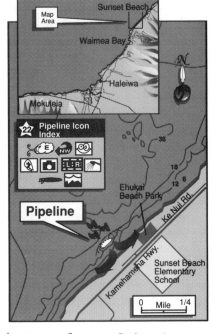

If you've ever seen an image of a wave at the Banzai Pipeline, it surely has burned itself into your mind's eye to haunt you forever. It doesn't matter whether it is a photo in a magazine, a sequence in a movie or terrifyingly up close in person, the effect is still the same: your soul is shaken. Whether it fills you with desire or dread, the image of a Pipeline tube is the most compelling sight in surfing.

Pipeline is the standard by which all other tubular waves are measured, as surfers describe a wave as either hollower than Pipeline, better than Pipeline, or less cavernous than Pipeline, but there is only one Pipeline.

Latching on to one of those eternal tubes is an event that can change your perspective on life. You will either become a true believer and life-long devotee, risking anything for just one more soul-searing visit to the tube, or a heretic who disdains the Pipe as just a quick barrel and not worth all the trouble.

Pipeline is the perfect arena for surfer and spectator alike. The waves break so close to the warm, soft, sandy beach that it puts life-threatening performances right in the laps of fascinated voyeurs. But your appreciation for the degree of danger changes as you move closer to the impact zone.

From high on the beach amphitheater the waves look exciting. From the edge of the water, they begin to look dangerous. From the safety of the channel the waves seem deadly, and from ground zero as a wave looms overhead about to explode on your head, it looks like certain death after prolonged torture.

The waves at Pipeline have a dangerously alluring appeal that draws

70

many more surfers out into the lineup than is safe. Although most surfers realize that an extremely shallow reef is responsible for Pipeline's coveted hollow dimensions, not enough of them contemplate what that means in terms of human pain and suffering. Pipeline probably would be spared the burden of such crushing crowds if the waves broke farther from shore, but since they break comfortingly close to a friendly beach, Pipeline is always swarming with surfers.

If you sit on the beach and watch long enough during a good swell, you will witness every depravity that man can commit against his fellow. One surfer will push himself over the ledge of the most insanely vertical wall, free-fall with only inches of rail holding him in, connect on the bottom and turn into a double overhead tube, only to have three guys blatantly drop in and stuff him into the pit for a dreadful walloping.

When the inevitable forest of tripods and cameras sprouts on the beach and the channel becomes clogged with water cameramen, the crowd in the waves is whipped into a frenzy that will inspire a surfer to gnaw off his best friend's arm just to get in the camera's viewfinder.

On a sunny day when the waves are small and fun, Pipeline is a nightmare of surfers and bodyboarders battling for the prime position on the best waves. The crowds scarcely diminish as the waves get bigger, but the danger level increases exponentially. About the only time you will get a wave to yourself at Pipeline is when the swell has menacing elements of north in it and the sandbar has built up on the inside, making each glorious takeoff end in a catastrophic closeout.

The best Pipeline surfers are the top predators of the surfing food chain, seizing the choicest waves and picking the carcasses clean, leaving other surfers only the scraps to quarrel over.

Hawaiian waves move with the speed of a striking death adder, making every take-off a possible adventure in free flight. Photo: Warren Bolster

When the Banzai Pipeline is in a generous mood it provides a double-barreled dose of fun through the Backdoor and front door. Photo: Warren Bolster

You might be wondering why anyone would submit themselves to so much abuse. It's only a wave, right? Ah, but what a wave. When it's 6 feet and under, Pipeline is the perfect energy field, with enough juice to make any maneuver possible: backside floaters atop the ledge that miraculously end in barrel rides, frantic free-falls from behind the peak that end up in a tube ride, or tube rides that end up with vicious lip assaults and whitewater rebounds.

Although the lefts start curling their lips in a snarl when the swell edges around to the north a bit, Backdoor Pipeline comes alive with gaping barrels. On the best days, surfers will divvy up the peak, with one surfer heading right and another left, each smug in the certainty that he will get tubed.

But while the rights are every bit as hollow as the lefts, there is a special torment that awaits surfers who try to feast on the tasty morsels Backdoor has to offer without paying for their repast. Since there is no channel for an easy return to the lineup, the waves at Backdoor deliver the kind of devastating punishment that should be reserved for only the most wicked sinners.

Praying won't help, and neither will begging for mercy. The best you can do is grit your teeth and whimper a little as the waves detonate and wrench your joints apart one ligament at a time. And to completely demoralize you, the waves will allow the fellow who was two strokes in front of you to duck under the same lip that slams you into the reef, even though you were paddling with inspired enthusiasm.

Rather than fool yourself into thinking you might be the lucky one to paddle straight back out and still escape punishment, you should let the white water carry you over past Pipeline and make the long, slow paddle back over to Backdoor.

As the waves get bigger, the surfing at Pipeline becomes stripped down to the essentials: get down, get in, get out. If you can add a bit of style to your ride, that's even better. There is something so supremely satisfying about turning yourself into God's own bullet as you load yourself into the celestial cylinder and let the wave blast you out of the muzzle.

But even with the ride reduced to such an elementary level, the potential for disaster is everywhere. The drop at Pipeline can make an Icarus of any surfer, giddy with excitement as he tries out his new wings. But like the ill-fated Icarus, many surfers crash and burn at Pipeline.

Fooling around at the Pipe when it's big is as perilous as kicking a sleeping wolverine: some of your favorite body parts could be chewed off. Every winter Pipeline maims and kills surfers whose only crime was trying to sample a little heaven on earth. After the roof caves in during your tube ride and you are swept away by the explosion, you will check your body in amazement that it could withstand such violence.

The best way not to become a victim is to know your limits before you paddle out. Although Pipeline is easily visible from lifeguard towers at Ke Waena and Ehukai staffed by the world's best life savers, disaster can occur before they can sprint up the beach to your assistance.

Study the surf carefully before you paddle out, and honestly appraise your chances of getting waves out there. Check out the crowd, swell direction, and outside sets, and then take stock of your equipment, ability and resolve. If they are deficient in any category, it might be good just to enjoy the action from the beach.

Watch the Pipeline regulars and you'll notice that to reach the lineup they walk up the beach toward Kaena Point until they are lined up with the crowd in the waves. Follow their example. Wait until a giant set is breaking and start scratching straight out. The rip will take you down the beach toward Ehukai, but just keep duck-diving under the white water until you can break through; then start stroking back toward the pack, savoring, in these last few moments of calm, the anticipation of the excitement and terror that await.

When you finally decide to make your move for a wave, you must paddle as though your life depends on catching it. It does.

The absolute worst place to be at Pipeline is stalled at the top when the lip throws out. You then become one with the lip, an exhilarating concept but a devastating reality.

All you can do is penetrate the water in a shallow dive and try to swim through the back. If you penetrate too deeply you'll get planted on the reef. If you don't swim vigorously enough through the back you'll get sucked over the falls from behind the wave, and slammed with enough force to compress every molecule of your being. If that happens, try to grab a breath of air as you head over the falls.

The second-worst place to be at Pipeline is caught inside, usually a result of not paddling enthusiastically enough for a wave and missing it. The best you can hope for here is to ditch your board, grab a deep breath and find a coral head or rock to cling to as the wave grabs you with unearthly force to drag you over the falls.

The third-worst place to be at Pipeline is inside an unmakable tube. One good way to dodge a body slam is to let the wave explode you out the back, and swim as rapidly away from the surge as possible to avoid a trip over the falls.

If you really dominate in the waves and begin to feel the need for a greater challenge, there is another horizon that awaits. When the swell pushes 15 feet and above, the outside reef wakes up and begins to hunger for surfers. But that's another story.

Rocky Point

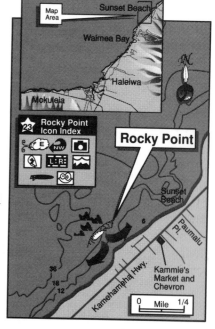

Location: Between Ehukai Beach Park and Sunset Beach
Activities: Shortboard surfing, bodyboarding
Wave: Fast performance right, hollow performance left
Difficulty: Intermediate to advanced surfers
Prime time: September through April
Wave range: West-northwest, northwest, north, northeast swells, 3-8 feet
Amenities: Parking, possible immortality on film

There are actually a few hours each winter when the rights and lefts at Rocky Point aren't mobbed by a frantic horde of surfers eager to become famous, and photographers happy to oblige them. The problem with the waves at Rocky Point is that they are so pretty that surfers become goofy in their ardor while courting these little flirts without skirts. The Rocky Point area is also favored as a living zone by visiting surfers, who are pleased to find such fine waves within walking distance.

The problem is further compounded because the waves are non-threatening and easy to rip, a refreshing change from many other North Shore power pits. Add a beach teeming with every photographic device known to man, and you create a frenzied surf zone that's fun for almost no one.

A meaty swell will batter Rocky Point and render it undridable, but swells 8 feet and under make this a hotdogger's heaven. This is the perfect wave magnet for attracting waves on rising or declining swells, and Rocky Point's value is increased because the waves will look lovely on a variety of wind directions, from northeast through southwest.

A more northerly swell arouses Rocky Rights and brings to life an assortment of nifty peelers that offer a smorgasbord of tube rides and multiple lip bashes.

With a heads-up pullout and some nimble paddling, you won't even be bothered by the lack of a channel on the rights. If you're caught inside, however, you might be given a graphic demonstration of how Rocky Point earned its name. While not as life-threatening as at other spots, the rocks and reef on the rights regularly collect skin and fiberglass samples in a clumsy and painful manner. But surfers derive their greatest nourishment from Rocky Point's lefts, which on a 5- to 8-foot northwest swell become canvasses waiting to be streaked with lip launches, snapbacks, aerials and floaters.

Anything is possible here, and the magazines and moviemakers rely on the inspired carefree contortions of riders blazing at Rocky Point to feed the fantasies of surfers everywhere.

Reality, however, has one nightmarish element.

Rocky Point is frequently as crowded as an Ethiopian refugee camp, and the surfers just as desperate. Your first impulse upon spotting a breeze-kissed overhead swell peeling perfectly at Rocky Point is to grab your board and paddle wildly into the lineup. But if you pause to watch for a few moments you'll notice that every wave is pounced upon and picked clean by at least a trio of hot surfers. Some of the world's most cunning wave snatchers end up getting burned on every wave at Rocky Point. Only you can determine where you fit into this equation, but the best way to find out is jump right in and try your luck.

Rocky Point is the essential North Shore experience for many visitors, who really didn't intend for their Hawaiian adventure to feature the fearsome waves and exhausting trouncings in the impact zone that other spots provide in such distressing abundance. Everybody rips at Rocky's. It's the place to cut loose and tap into Hawaiian juice without putting your life on the line.

The speed of the waves on the rights and lefts provides the energy to launch into some maniacally inspired maneuvers, and while the wipeouts can be painful, they lack the serious menace of most other North Shore spots.

Another aspect that enhances Rocky Point's status as a superior surf site is the bevy of lovely lasses that blossom like a garland of flowers on the sand.

If the action in the waves is too frenzied for your taste, you can always kick back on the beach and enjoy the performance in the lineup and the scenery on the sand. Parking is available along Kamehameha Highway and Ke Nui Road. One public right of way across the street from a giant wood carving of a Hawaiian with a rock perched atop his head (no kidding) gives the best view of the rights. Another right of way about 200 yards toward Sunset Beach offers access to the lefts.

Don't keep anything in your car that you are emotionally attached to, as it will quickly become the cherished possession of the fast-fingered set.

There is a channel off a sandy cove that makes paddling out to the lefts simple and painless, and allows you the luxury of pausing to admire other surfers' rides before powering out to perform your own heroics.

Surfers hoping to work their magic on the rights are in for a more difficult entry. While you can paddle out through the channel on the lefts and head down to the rights, that long route becomes wearisome after a few long strokes. Wade out on the shallow reef flat and time the set; then start paddling when the biggest set is breaking, and don't stop for anything. Most surfers on the rights kick out on the fly and hit the water paddling to avoid getting smacked by the rest of the set. If you wipe out or straighten out on a closeout, your path back to the waves will involve running the gauntlet of battering waves.

Remember that it will all be worth it when you get back out: one of the many surf photographers infesting the beach and water is bound to mistake you for someone famous and confer limited celluloid immortality upon you.

Backyards

Location: Around the corner from Sunset Beach
Activities: Shortboard surfing, sailboarding
Wave: Stunningly fast right, powerful left
Difficulty: Advanced to expert surfers
Prime time: September through April
Wave range: West-northwest, northwest, north swells, 5-10 feet, northwest is best
Amenities: Parking, amazing windsurfing action

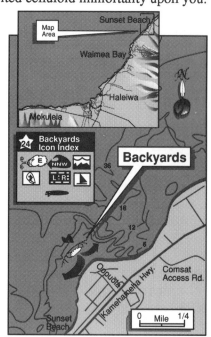

Just when you think the waves couldn't possibly get any more crowded, another planeload of surfers arrives and inspires you to contemplate giving up surfing for a less frustrating endeavor.

Other surfers deal with the crowds by abandoning the prime-time surf spots for seldom-surfed locations. Usually, however, those spots are seldom surfed because they aren't very good, or are much more dangerous than the prime spots. Such is the case with Backyards. This is a brutal surf spot for rugged surfers.

Ever so seldom, when the wind and the tide and the swell and the moon and the planets and the stars are in harmony, you can actually have some fun surfing Backyards. Usually, however, Backyards provides the kind of adventure that leaves you gratefully marvelling that you escaped with so few serious injuries. These surly waves devote their brief lives to bashing surfers. (Windsurfers are agile enough to escape the full fury of the waves, which only goads the waves into venting their frustration on the slower surfers.)

There are those surfers who crave the kind of painful excitement to be found while surfing Backyards, and it is a bonus that they will never have to battle crowds to satisfy their cravings.

The reef is a dreaded guardian at Backyards, and has compiled a gruesome collection of surfer skin over the years. The reef is black with sea urchins, which only help the coral inflict pain on human trespassers. No matter that you only want to take some pleasure from the ocean during your surf session, the reef will make you pay for your fun.

The wave explodes on the shallow reef, and the many peaks that comprise the lineup at Backyards are erratic. It will be a supreme test of your paddling and wave judgment to find the sweet spot in the lineup as the waves shift and peak up tauntingly just beyond your reach.

The wave at Backyards expects no mercy and gives none, but it will jump-start your heart and get your adrenaline flowing. Photo: Warren Bolster

If you opt to ride the lefts, you at least have a rudimentary if shallow and narrow channel to help you get back to the lineup. But the rights break more often than the lefts, and since there is no channel to provide safe passage, the paddle back out for another wave can punish you far beyond anything that your possible past misdeeds might have earned you.

Getting caught inside on the rights is as paralyzing as being trapped in a nerve gas factory explosion. But after a session at Sunset where every superstar, hotshot and stooge in the world is either ripping you off or bumbling around in the way, the empty peaks at Backyards seem worth any possible pounding that hollow waves and shallow reef can dish out.

Backyards is best on an easterly wind, southeasterly wind or no wind at all. With a solid northwest swell, the rights can line up for a speed run that asks no quarter and gives none, but just might provide a thrill a minute. While the lefts don't begin to match Pipeline's perfect barrels, they do make up for it by providing long, rippable sections and hidden hollow treats with none of Pipeline's maddening crowds.

To get to Backyards, turn down Oopuola Street off Kamehameha Highway just east of Sunset Beach, and look for parking on one of the side streets. The beach parking lot is for a local sailboard club, which vigilantly maintains its parking exclusivity at the lot.

An alternative is to park at Sunset Beach and make the long walk around the point, which is enlivened by giving you a closeup view of the action at Sunset while you trudge to Backyards.

The best way to reach the lineup is to paddle through the channel straight off the windsurfers' parking lot, and head down to the rights. When you are caught inside by the ceaseless set from Hell that won't let you claw back out through the waves, you can either paddle over to the channel at the lefts, or make the long paddle to Sunset and back around the point. Both options can drain your energy reserves pretty quickly, but are usually preferable to getting worked over by Mother Ocean's bodyguards.

Windsurfers have swooped down on Backyards and taken it over, deeming it the island's most thrilling wave-jumping location. Although the wind helps sailboarders out of situations that would trounce a surfer, the ordeal of being pounded by waves while trying to save your mast, boom, sail and board puts the lie to the saying "No brains, no headaches."

Backyards has plenty of headaches for everyone, brainless or otherwise. If you are surfing on a marginal day when the windsurfers descend, or are beached by howling winds and giant waves, it might be worth your while to stick around at Backyards and enjoy the show. These wave-jumping fools that call themselves the Yardbirds will put on a demonstration of athletic ability and disregard for danger that will leave you stupefied.

Velzyland

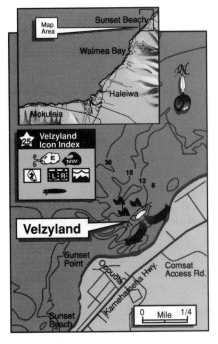

Location: Last spot on North Shore, Kahuku from Sunset Point
Activities: Shortboard surfing, body-boarding, sailboarding on outside reef
Wave: Ultra-hollow right and long left
Difficulty: Intermediate and advanced surfers
Prime time: September through April
Wave range: West-northwest, north-west, north, northeast swells 3-7 feet, best on northwest
Amenities: None

You could dedicate your life to a worldwide search, but you wouldn't find a more thrilling small-wave surf spot than Velzyland. After one tube at V-Land, most surfers are in love for life. Velzyland is a wave factory that churns out the thrills all winter long. Even when the big swells come sweeping in, if you look closely you can usually find a small group of wily veterans out riding the re-formed inside section.

Because of a lucky arrangement of the mountains and canyons, the wind will blow offshore at Velzyland while other North Shore spots are in tatters. It's a good bet to check V-Land on any swell before making the rounds of the other spots, as you will seldom be disappointed.

This wave can make all your surf dreams come true. The outside peak jacks up for an insane drop, followed by a flat section that lets you gather your wits and plan your assault on the inside bowl. It's an amazing phenomenon of physics that permits the inside reef to transform a 3-foot wave into a tube hollow enough to accommodate a 300-pound bruddah, but that's what V-Land is all about: gaping barrels.

Even a mushy peak will be magically altered into a hollow Oh!!! of exclaimation when it encounters the shallow inside section, turning an average wave into another portal to the tubular realm.

Every portion of the wave is explored with creativity, with surfers pulling off floaters and aerials with ruinous disregard for the waiting reef. On a good day you will see unspeakable things done to waves, which just might inspire you to a new level of performance.

When the left is working, it acts as a pressure valve on the packed rights and provides some long and workable walls. Although shunned by many surfers who would rather battle for the rights, the lefts can be as good as those at Rocky Point. The penalty for indulging in a left, however, is a grueling paddle back to the lineup over a shallow reef with no channel.

Unfortunately, Velzyland has some problems that can take it from the status of surf fantasy to surf disaster. The takeoff zone is narrow enough to force surfers to rub elbows, which is like cramming pit bulls into a pen and tossing in some meat.

The best way to snag waves is to ditch the pack and either hang out on the Kahuku side of the lineup for the lefts, or linger near the inside section and pounce when someone gets mauled on takeoff or while attempting a wildly improbable maneuver. Foot for foot, this is the most powerful wave on Oahu. You will surface gasping after being violated by a 4-foot wave, astounded by the evil violence contained in such a small package.

You could more easily escape being scratched by an angry cat stuffed into your surf trunks than to complete a session at Velzyland unscathed by the sharp, shallow reef. As your numerous cuts slowly heal you will have plenty of time to brood on how much higher the pain factor could be increased if the reef at V-Land could handle a 10-foot swell.

Velzyland remains an honest wave in an era of hype and flash. Drop in, get tubed and make it, or get worked by the reef. Photo: Denjiro Sato

But Velzyland's 3- to 7-foot surly little power bombs already manage to pass out a disproportionate amount of punishment, although apparently not enough to keep the crowds away.

Not a single wave goes unridden, and the cunning pack of surfers that patrols Velzyland is so slick they will trick you out of your surf shorts, then paddle up and casually ask to borrow your wax. The regulars are always in the right spot, always get the deepest tubes and take the most radical chances, usually with mind-blowing success.

The previously thief-plagued parking lot has been turned into paved roads for a planned housing development, and the access gate is always locked. Parking is possible along Kamehameha Highway, or on nearby Kaunala Place or Iwia Place.

There is another lot that gives a great view from the lefts but is quickly filled. Turn onto a dirt road beside the University of Hawaii livestock research farm along Kamehameha Highway just past the last houses and turn left at the junction.

The best access to the lineup is through a small channel straight ashore from the lineup. Although tiny, the channel is well developed and a great path to the waves at low tide. Another good route is to paddle out in the deeper water about 30 yards toward Sunset from the inside section.

On days when Velzyland is too small to accommodate even the slightest grommet in its tubes, bodyboarders will find the waves overhead, and perfect for their prone antics. Bodyboarding is also fun at V-Land when the waves are bigger, but the surfers form a fairly intimidating force.

And when the swell really buries the reef in an avalanche of white water, an outside reef makes a serious playground for sailboarders. Definitely not for anyone who prefers to be able to see the shore from the lineup.

Filmmaker Bruce Brown would probably be aghast at the vicious crowds that infest the spot he so whimsically named after shaper Dale Velzy back in the '50s. But on a good day when that special section gapes invitingly and you gaze in wonder from the inside looking out, you just might be as inspired as the graffitist who carved "Velzyland Forever" on the bridge ashore.

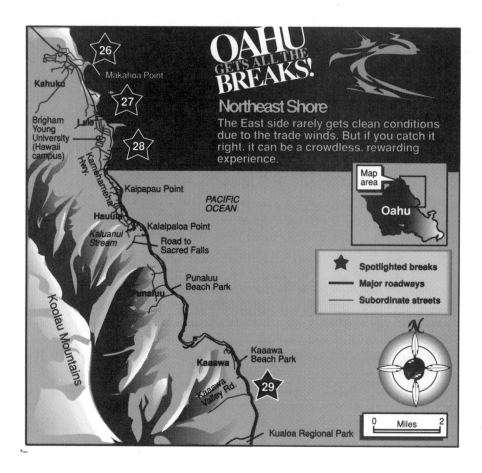

OAHU GETS ALL THE BREAKS!

Northeast Shore

The East side rarely gets clean conditions due to the trade winds. But if you catch it right, it can be a crowdless, rewarding experience.

Makahoa Point

Kahuku

Brigham Young University (Hawaii campus)

Laie

Kamehameha Hwy.

26

27

28

Kaipapau Point

PACIFIC OCEAN

Hauula

Kaluanui Stream

Kalaipaloa Point

Road to Sacred Falls

Punaluu Beach Park

Punaluu

Koolau Mountains

Kaaawa Beach Park

Kaaawa

Kaaawa Valley Rd.

29

Kualoa Regional Park

Map area

Oahu

★ Spotlighted breaks

━━ Major roadways

━━ Subordinate streets

N

0 Miles 2

Seventh Hole

Location: Off the 7th hole of the Kahuku Golf Course
Activities: Shortboard surfing
Wave: Booming left peak, short right
Difficulty: Intermediate to advanced surfers
Prime time: Best September through April, breaks all year
Wave range: East, northeast, north, north-northwest or huge northwest swells, 4-10 feet, northeast is best
Amenities: Parking, relative isolation

One of the best reasons for setting foot on a golf course can be found in Kahuku. If you can safely pass the gauntlet of golf balls whizzing past as you cross the fairway on the 7th hole, you might be rewarded by a splendid sight: beautiful, big lefts peeling into a deep-water channel.

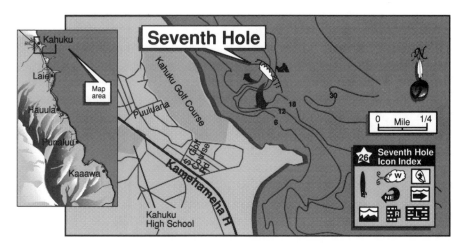

Before the Turtle Bay condominiums were built and rented to visiting surfers, this area was seldom surfed. Although it's still a natural wonderland, good swells here now are sometimes packed with visitors and residents alike.

A gratifying variety of winter swells find their way to the reefs of 7th Hole, from huge northwest swells wrapping around Kahuku Point to smaller north and northeast swells funneling straight into the lineup.

This should be one of your first stops when a bull of a swell overpowers the North Shore and sends you scurrying elsewhere for ridable waves.

Smaller swells hit the reef and create a right/left combination, with the lefts peeling into a deep channel while the rights end up on the reef. As the swells pump up in bulk, the rights get slammed shut while the lefts attain epic proportions.

Unfortunately, the prevailing trade winds hide the waves under a veil of ugliness that no one is willing to peek beneath. That veil is lifted only when glassy, windless conditions or westerly kona breezes apply their artful cosmetics to make the waves look desirable.

But when conditions are right, surfing 7th Hole is an invigorating experience. Looking at the wild shoreline from the distant lineup, you can fantasize that you are surfing some exotic spot in the untamed surfing world.

This area maintains a splendid isolation that is increasingly rare as each little nook on Oahu is discovered and developed. Surfing here is a wilderness experience to savor before economic enhancement reduces it to a memory.

Under 6 feet, the rights and lefts are playfully willing to tolerate any frenzied surfing indignity you care to impose on them. The waves regain their dignity as they increase in size, until at 8 to 10 feet they endure only the most adept surfers carving the most serious lines.

The punishment for failure to approach the bigger waves with respect is swift and severe, usually involving a vigorous full-body saltwater massage that makes you wonder whether your appendages will be of any use to you when the wave has finished its painful therapy.

Waves come charging out of deep water and arch and pitch when they hit the shallow reef. The resulting left will help give you a graphic image for the vague ideas you might have about power.

You can save yourself a world of misery if you find some dependable landmarks on the beach to line up with to keep the sets from ambushing you out of position. Each wave starts as an ill-defined lump of energy that is rapidly transformed into a liquid cliff, so every takeoff is an exercise in free flight.

You have to plan your moves with laser speed, as the wave zips along and rewards indecision with a solid thumping. Each wave is fiercely independent, and asserts its right to break on a whim. While the first wave of a set might be a fiberglass-melting speed-run tube from start to finish, the next few waves could feature surprise caverns and slow sections perfect for fancy carving maneuvers.

With easterly elements to the swell, the rights will seduce you with a steep peak and fast, well-formed wall. The ride will be so enjoyable that you might momentarily forget that there is no channel for a safe return trip to the pleasure zone. The rest of the set will offer a painful reminder.

Many times it's a good plan to ride the white water over to the channel off the lefts and paddle back around to the rights. Unfortunately, prolonged contact with the reef does nothing to diminish the power of these waves, and the white water can kidnap you for a runaway ride to the inside shelf. Just relax and enjoy it, and try to angle over to the channel.

Although the channel is deep enough to provide a safe entrance to and exit from the surf zone, a wipeout can leave you far from the safety of the beach in an area of shallow reef surging with strong rip currents. The best plan is to relax and help the currents carry you toward the channel so you can catch your breath as you plan a new assault on the waves.

Luckily, if the unthinkable happens, Kahuku Hospital is only minutes away and physicians there have vast experience in reassembling surfers.

As you pass through Kahuku town, turn onto Puuluana Street across from Kahuku High. At a fork in the road a left turn will take you to the Kahuku Golf Course clubhouse. Follow the road until you find a parking area with a view of the waves. The peak at 7th Hole will be to your extreme right, and a walk up the beach a few hundred yards will take you to the channel.

If you continue along Kamehameha Highway, turn left across the street from the Catholic church. Park near the south end of the fairways and slip across the greens and you will find yourself atop a sand dune with one of the great views in all of surfing. The peak and channel will be spread out at your feet, making it easy to fantasize yourself on the waves.

Just remember as you cross the golf course that you are trespassing, and some golfers might enjoy the challenge of hitting a moving target.

South Golf Course Road will also get you into the parking area, as will Adams Road, which will take you to the back side of the softball fields, another good place to park.

The best path to the lineup is across a short but shallow limestone shelf and into a deeper lagoon that leads to the channel. With any luck the rip will haul you out to the waves. The rest is up to you.

Unless you foolishly try to battle the channel to the beach, the waves will give you a welcome burst of speed to shore. The last few yards are shallow and the coral sharp, so move with care.

If you're looking for fame and fortune, you'll never find it at 7th Hole. The photogs are too busy infesting the Pipeline to wander into this rough wilderness, and the only things you'll find at 7th Hole are adventure and splendid, solitary surfing.

Goat Island

Location: Off Malaekahana State Park
Activities: Shortboard surfing, bodyboarding, sailboarding
Wave: Long series of left peaks with hollow sections
Difficulty: Beginning to advanced surfers
Prime time: Best September through April, breaks all year
Wave range: North, northeast, east-northeast, east, and giant northwest swells, 3-7 feet
Amenities: Parking, showers, restrooms

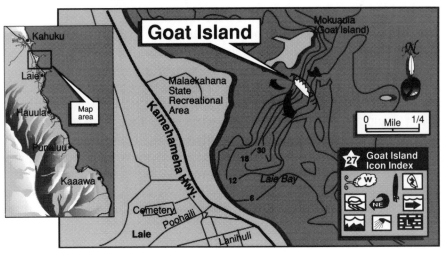

The sleepy little town of Laie is the site of Oahu's North Shore surfer refuge off Goat Island.

Even though swells continue to visit the North Shore during the long, hot summer months, they aren't frequent or ferocious enough to satisfy the voracious appetites of the North Shore's resident surfers. Some surfers sate their ravenous wave cravings by adventuring to foreign shores, but not everyone can afford such an indulgence. So to ease their surf hunger, the island-bound wave hunters frequently forage off Goat Island, where the constant trade winds produce waves all year.

You won't find any goats on Goat Island, since the herds that the Mormon settlers of Laie banished to Mokuauia Island because of their destructive behavior ashore died out years ago.

The island is still witness to some aberrant behavior as surfers whack the tops off of waves and generally create mayhem on these juicy walls. Although the waves off Goat Island can get your attention with an abrupt saltwater head slap and the coral can leave painful tattoos on your carcass, this usually is a nonthreatening surf zone.

A reef stretches from the east side of Goat Island and angles off to deep water, creating a series of pitching peaks that can connect on northeasterly swells. If you snare one of these endless sidewinders, you will have a glimpse of insight into why so many people are so fond of Goat Island.

This is not a wave for unimaginative surfers who demand boringly predictable sections. These lefts will test your creativity and ability to instantly improvise. If your surfing style calls to mind Beethoven's 5th rather than Joe Satriani's riffs, you will be maddened by Goat Island's shifting peaks and ambushing hollow sections. But if your technique makes people hear the late great Stevie Ray Vaughan as they watch you in action, you'll be able to create some truly wild tracks on the walls here.

The waves come sweeping out of cobalt blue deep water and hit the reef in a sky-scraping leap that makes the drop an adventure in aerodynamics. The wall will either open up and swallow you, or hold back long enough to let you lay down some good lines, then swallow you on the inside section.

As you paddle out, decide which peak is calling your name, and stick with it though the session. Otherwise you can graze through the whole lineup and grab whichever wave is closest, sampling the delights of each section.

The wind is a major factor here, as the same trades that kick up the waves also make them ugly. But if the trades aren't too brisk, the waves are very ridable. When kona winds are blowing, the waves are downright delectable, as the walls become smoother and the tubes deeper and more accommodating. The waves are also delicious during glassy land-breeze mornings and evening glass-offs.

There is plenty of parking for Goat Island, but getting a parking spot can be a problem on those rewarding dawn patrols. Access is through Malaekahana State Park, which doesn't open until 7 a.m. When the gate does open, park in the first lot and scramble down to the beach to check the waves.

If you're ready to rip before the gate is open, you can always park at nearby Hukilau Beach Park and walk up the shore until you get to Goat Island, a walk that may be tedious but is much better than going crazy waiting for Malaekahana's gates to be opened.

The two best methods to reach the waves are completely different. The easiest way is to paddle the short distance between the park and the island, and walk along the island's shore to a good jumping spot. Then time the sets and launch into the waves, and stroke like mad. This technique allows you to tow out a cooler full of food and drinks to stash on the island to help recharge your batteries between sessions.

The other route is to paddle from the beach closer to Laie and skirt the reef, then make the long stroke in deeper water. The advantage here is that you can plot your attack on the waves as you paddle out, and even snag a few stragglers.

The island is a bird refuge, and site of some wanton cruelty where the nesting wedge-tailed shearwaters have been slaughtered. Although the state places the island off limits after each batch of killings, it cautiously reopens it eventually. Treat these animals with consideration and you'll help keep the island open to visitors.

About the only menacing aspect of Goat Island is an occasional invasion of Portuguese man-of-wars. While not as deadly as a trip over the falls at Pipeline, these little blue devils can significantly alter your enjoyment level in the waves. As you walk along the beach before paddling out, check to see if the fleet is in town. If there are no blue bodies covering the shore, paddle out and have fun. Otherwise, count the corpses, check the waves and decide whether it's worth the risk.

PCC (Polynesian Cultural Center)

Location: Across from the Polynesian Cultural Center in Laie
Activities: Shortboard surfing, bodyboarding
Wave: Fast, long lefts, often hollow; short rights
Difficulty: Intermediate to advanced surfers
Prime time: Best September through April, breaks all year
Wave range: North, northeast, east-northeast, east, and giant northwest swells, 3-8 feet
Amenities: Parking along Kamehameha Highway, no crowds

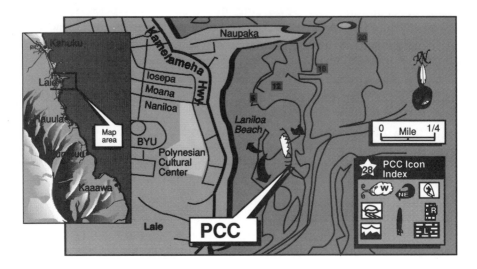

Sometimes the very things that drive you crazy can bring you happiness. One of the eternal problems in surfing is access to those liquid objects of our desires. What good does it do you to know that perfect waves are breaking if you can't reach them?

In Laie there is one miserable public right-of-way for more than a mile of coastline, a situation that keeps surfers from pausing for a surf check as they cruise down the highway on their wave hunt. But for those who don't mind risking the ire of angry homeowners, there is a treasure hiding beyond the No Trespassing signs.

In the middle of the bay is a peak that will make every cell in your body ache with desire if you see it when it's going off. Under the prime conditions of kona wind and a solid 6-foot northeast swell, PCC is a vision of loveliness. The wave hits the reef and throws out in a screaming hollow cavern that zips along for 200 yards.

It doesn't matter whether you tackle these waves frontside or backside, the thrill will be the same. At higher tide the waves flatten out a bit and provide a suitable surface for serious carving. But at low tide you'll be treated to significant time in the tube, with an occasional slow section for a floater or lip bash.

As the swell swings around more to the east, the rights begin to become more than a momentary diversion from the lefts as they start to strive with the lefts in a battle to lure you over to their side of the peak. But after savoring a long, hollow ride on the rights, you'll want to head back to the lineup with some fervent stroking, as the lack of a channel can let the rest of the set have its way with you.

If you took a dozen visiting surfers and tossed them into the waves at

PCC, after a few irksome hours they would deem these peaks the most vexing waves they have ever encountered. The source of this frustration is a reef about 40 yards outside the lineup that delights in tormenting surfers. As the bigger set waves approach, they hit this outside reef and jack up, tricking all but the most disciplined surfers into sprinting from their inside lineup in a frantic attempt to avoid or snag these outside sets.

Don't be so easily duped. These peaks just cap over and mush out, while the wave reforms inside for a long barrel that will seemingly taunt you as you watch in bewilderment from way too far outside. By holding your position when these devious sets approach, you can smirk as the less alert surfers scramble outside, confident that they will be forced to watch as you rip the waves they just missed.

When giant northwest swells batter the North Shore, or coveted north, northeast or east swells coincide with kona winds or glassy conditions, it's time to start roaming the Windward side seeking uncrowded waves. You'll be cheating yourself out of a savory experience if you pass up Laie.

As you start cursing the absence of checkout spots, just remember that this lack of access is what keeps PCC uncrowded. The only legal path to the beach is a city and county access trail located about 500 yards north of McDonald's. You can also find access to the waves through empty lots, or houses that look as though they aren't patrolled by dogs. Just remember to be discreet, since you are trespassing, and most people hate the idea of surfers skulking through their yard. Luckily, the residents of Laie are friendly and usually will allow you to pass through to the waves.

The beach here is long and sandy, with a lagoon on the southern portion and a shallow coral shelf fronting the entire stretch of coast. The best route to the waves is to wade carefully across the coral shelf and paddle out just south of where the lefts quietly expire, keeping a sharp eye out for coral heads that can appear without warning.

Parking is possible along Kamehameha Highway after lining up your access to the ocean, usually within sight of the Polynesian Cultural Center. Once you make it to the beach, check out the waves and plan your path to the takeoff area, seeking the line of least resistance around the breaking waves.

Once you make it out to the fun zone, the most reliable lineup is the roof of one of the Polynesian Cultural Center's structures. With your lineup helping keep you on top of the surf action, you can let your attention wander between sets and enjoy one of the most sublime views on Oahu.

With so much of the island covered by large structures and dwellings, it's a treat to surf in a place where the lack of crowds and the lack of development can provide a tiny taste of what it must have been like to ride the waves before surfing and Hawaii became too distressingly congested.

Kanenelu Beach

Location: Between Kaaawa and Kualoa
Activities: Shortboard surfing, longboard surfing, bodyboarding, wave skiing
Wave: Fun right walls, some lefts
Difficulty: Beginning to intermediate surfers
Prime time: Best September through April, breaks all year
Wave range: North, northeast, east swells, 2-6 feet
Amenities: Parking along Kamehameha Highway

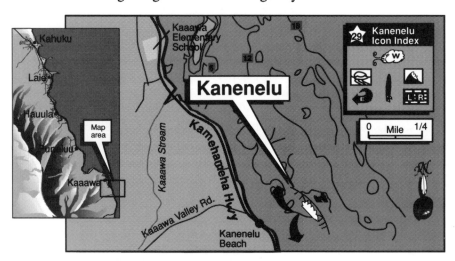

Kanenelu is a delightful sight after you travel Kamehameha Highway the length of Kaneohe Bay without a glimpse of the ocean, let alone waves. And after a few weeks of battering by the North Shore's winter waves, Kanenelu is a welcome change. It is also a great backup when the summer South Shore is coy and waveless, and provides a fun assortment of waves all year long.

When winter swells are blasting the North Shore's spots to oblivion, the swell frequently wraps around and reaches the Windward coast in surfable form. By the time the waves reach Kanenelu, the fear factor has been drained from them, leaving friendly waves perfect for a relaxing surf session.

North, northeast and east swells hit the reef in full force, coercing the waves into a limp imitation of the North Shore's small-wave specialty spots. Add a kona wind or early morning glass to these easterly swells, and the rights can clean up their act and perform their Velzyland impersonation, though they can't quite seem to copy Velzyland's super hollow dimensions.

When wind, swell and tide come together, Kanenelu can provide a stimulating session. But the trade winds usually batter the spirit out of the waves, leaving peaks more suitable for longboarders, bodyboarders and beginners.

The same trade winds that beat up the waves here also create waves, making Kanenelu a surf factory that produces all year long. Even though the waves won't keep you awake nights savoring the memory of each hollow section and thrilling wall, they do provide a ton of fun for many people.

Parking is plentiful along Kamehameha Highway, and nonsurfers in the group can fish, picnic, beachcomb, and swim at the white sandy beach.

A main peak toward the point from the beach hoards the best action, while other sections of the reef provide uncrowded peaks for bodyboarders, beginners, wave-skiers and others too shy to grapple with the pack at the main peak. Access to the waves is easy from the sandy beach, and you can anticipate an unstressful session free from coral cuts or punishing waves.

Many surfers incorrectly call this spot Kuloa, a mispronunciation of nearby Kualoa Point and Kualoa Beach Park, but whatever you call it, the waves here are fun for everyone.

Makapuu

Location: Makapuu Beach Park
Activities: Bodysurfing, bodyboarding, limited surfing
Wave: Long left peaks, pounding shorebreak
Difficulty: Beginners to experts
Prime time: Biggest September through April, breaks all year
Wave range: All swells with any east, 2-12 feet
Amenities: Parking, restrooms, lifeguard, showers, excellent scenery

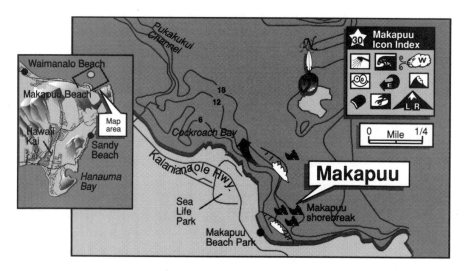

Your mama always told you there would be days when you wouldn't be able to find a wave good enough to inspire you to drag your board into the ocean, but she never told you what to do about it.

However, she'd probably nod happily if she heard someone advising you to head for Makapuu Beach Park. On those maddening days when you just can't find some surf worth dipping your stick into even though you are crazed with desire to immerse yourself in some salt water, Makapuu will probably save your sanity.

It's difficult to imagine another ocean playground that can show so many people such a good time as often as Makapuu does, and in such an exciting setting. On those rare occasions when the waves avoid even Makapuu's reefs and sandbars, it is one of life's gentle pleasures to bask on the sand, entranced by the view of the lighthouse on the rugged cliffs, and break free from your meditation for refreshing plunges in the ocean.

If you're really lucky, you might be entertained by those air-brained daredevils who leap from the jagged Koolau cliffs to soar in long, lazy loops in their hang gliders.

But the waves seldom desert these favored shores. During the summer when Town hasn't seen a ridable wave in weeks, demented surfers abandon their boards and descend upon Makapuu to soak up the energy from the trade-wind-borne swells.

Summertime is also prime time for crowd watching, as Makapuu becomes a haven for an assortment of interesting beachgoers.

In the summer, the ocean is in a playful mood, with sunny skies and sparkling blue waves calling surfers to come frolic and inviting giddy visitors and children to splash in the small shorebreak waves.

Many bodyboarders head to the outside peak to spin themselves dizzy with continuous whirligig 360s on the slow left peak, ending in a quick tube and brief pounding in the shorebreak.

Other bodysurfers and bodyboarders lurk in the shorebreak, addicted to the savage fun of the fast tubes and saltwater massages in the shore pound.

The beach assumes a grim countenance during the winter, with cold winds whipping giant waves breaking under gray skies, and fierce currents surging through the ocean. On these days the hesitant surfers line the cliff-top lookout while only the world's top bodyboarders challenge the surf, and the lifeguards really earn their pay.

The wide sandy beach of summer is sucked away by these powerful waves, laying bare fangs of lava that can dramatically disrupt rides in the shorebreak. But the winter also brings some seriously fine days of good waves and astounding bodyboard and bodysurfing action.

When the waves begin to push over the 4-foot level, you should pause before you plunge into the water and assess your endurance and swimming ability. The currents created by these waves move relentlessly out to sea south toward the lighthouse or north toward Waimanalo, and are strong enough to exhaust a barracuda. Don't even think of tackling these waves without a good pair of swim fins unless you want the current to treat you to a free trip to Kauai.

Although Makapuu is enjoyed by hordes of people every day, parking is seldom a problem. If you are lucky enough to find a spot in the lower lots, you will save yourself a few steps to the ocean. Just make sure you lock your car and leave anything you are fond of at home. Despite the high-profile presence of uniformed Honolulu police officers, these lower lots get worked over regularly by thieves.

Otherwise, there is plenty of parking on both sides of Kalanianaole Highway, with numerous paths leading down the cliff to the beach. Use the cliff-top perspective to line up the best peak so you know where to paddle once you hit the water.

Many local surfers demonstrate their daring by diving into the waves from the lava rocks at the north end of the bay. This impressive display is far more difficult than it looks, and requires excellent timing and agility. If you lack both, you just might end up planting your face in the lava as the wave recedes and getting slammed by the next wave.

Most people prefer to enter the water along the beach, duck under the shorebreak waves and stroke for the outside peak, paying close attention to the power and direction of the current.

When the state Department of Transportation finally tired of hearing complaints from bodysurfers who were being run over by surfers, it created a surfboard-free sanctuary where bodysurfers, bodyboarders and swimmers can cavort without worrying about unplanned amateur surgery by surfboards. The lifeguards vigorously defend Makapuu against invasion by surfers on boards.

Fortunately, the ban doesn't extend around the point toward Waimanalo, where one of the Windward coast's best surf spots still welcomes a challenge from surfers on boards. With a good east-southeast, east or northeast swell and either kona winds or glassy conditions, this lava ledge will treat you to a surf adventure you'll remember long after less exciting sessions have faded from your memory banks.

Waves hit the jagged shelf and pitch in a full-bore, surfer-gobbling right tube that winds from beginning to end. The technique to keep from being stomped into the shelf is to decide before you start paddling for a wave that you really, really, really want to catch it. As the wave sucks out and jacks up, take a few more fevered strokes and drop in at an angle, and keep pumping for the shoulder.

If the swell is hitting right, you can spend the entire ride from takeoff to pullout in the tube. When the wind, swell or tide aren't favorable, the wave flattens out a bit and allows nonessential moves such as turns, lip bashes and cutbacks, but the penalty for not making a wave is always the same: a painful trip over the shelf.

The most clever route back to the lineup when you're caught inside is to avoid a useless frontal-assault battle against the waves and instead let the white water carry you over the shelf to the deeper water.

To get to this spot, just take the campground access road across from the back entrance to Sea Life Park and station your car with a good view of the lineup. Check the waves and time the sets; then make your way down to the water and launch off the lava into the deeper water where the waves peter out.

Whether you are looking for a soothing session on a hot summer day or a serious challenge during a wild winter swell, Makapuu is waiting to show you a good time.

Rabbit Island

Location: Offshore of Makapuu Beach Park
Activities: Shortboard surfing, longboard surfing, wave-skiing
Wave: Fast performance right, sometimes hollow
Difficulty: Intermediate to advanced surfers
Prime time: Best September through April, breaks all year
Wave range: North, northeast, east swell, 4-8 feet, north is best
Amenities: Unique surfing experience

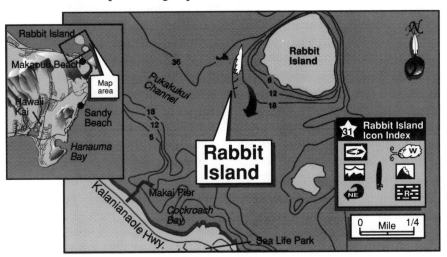

As America's best surfing sites have been forced to host increasing numbers of surfers as the population flocks the coasts, it has become increasingly difficult to find a true surf adventure close to home. And yet, you can find one within sight of one of Oahu's most popular and crowded beaches.

If you let your imagination take over, when you look at Rabbit Island just offshore of Makapuu Beach Park you can see a bunny up to his nose in the ocean and eternally swimming with his ears laid back, dipping into the sea. And if you know what you're looking for, in a solid north or northeast swell you can see waves peeling off right where the rabbit's ears touch the water.

Manana Island has been called Rabbit Island ever since some enterprising Waimanalo farmer tried to raise rabbits on this barren island, only to have the little bunnies perish of thirst.

When a 6-foot swell hits the shelf on the north end of the island, the waves pitch out and peel as they bend around the tip. It's one of surfing's most curious sensations to be sitting off an island far from shore trying to ride waves as they bend and break straddling a shallow shelf and deep water.

Many surfers prefer waves that break comfortingly close to shore and are unnerved as they wait for sets in the cobalt blue, frighteningly deep water that creates such a wide psychological barrier all the way to the distant beach.

That unease only helps keep Rabbit Island from being overrun by surfers on good swells. The long paddle from shore is also daunting, and ensures that only the truly daring earn the reward of uncrowded waves.

Countless surfers have been driven mad by the sight of Rabbit Island's waves peeling alluringly on a glassy day because they weren't willing to invest any time or energy in paddling to reach those distant peaks.

While most north, northeast and east swells create waves off Rabbit Island, only kona winds or glassy conditions let the waves reach their full potential and make them desirable enough to justify the tremendous effort necessary to reach them. But surfers will disregard angry, armed guards when in the grip of wave lust, and a long paddle over deep water shouldn't be enough to keep determined surfers from an adventure at Rabbit Island.

The simplest way to reach Rabbit Island's beckoning walls is to park near the University of Hawaii Makai Laboratory, walk to the end of the pier and start stroking. The paddle is only about twice as far as the paddle out to Threes in Waikiki, and a bigger board makes the distance fly by. One good trick is to paddle a tanker and tow your shortboard by its leash, and stash the tanker on Rabbit Island until you've caught your share of waves and are ready for the long paddle back to shore.

Of course, the ultimate voyage to Rabbit Island is by boat, but not everyone packs a twin-outboard Merc speedster when they're hunting waves. If you've got some cash or are pretty persuasive, however, you might be able to wangle yourself a ride with fishermen. Keep a sharp lookout as you cruise through Waimanalo for fishermen preparing to launch their boat, and see if you can't work out a deal. Otherwise, head for the Koko Marina in Hawaii Kai and walk the docks in search of a departing fisherman or pleasure boater, or wait by the launching facilities at Maunalua Bay Beach Park and see if you can't find a reasonable boater.

No matter what route you take to enjoy Rabbit Island's alluring peaks, it's well worth the effort to enjoy one of the last real surf adventures in America.

Sandy Beach

Location: Fronting Sandy Beach Park
Activities: Shortboard surfing, bodysurfing, bodyboarding, sand-sliding
Wave: Hollow, booming shorebreak peaks, performance peaks on outside reefs
Difficulty: Beginner to expert surfers
Prime time: Best April through September, breaks all year
Wave range: All swells with any south, 2-10 feet
Amenities: Parking, showers, restrooms, lifeguards, incredible action close to shore, interesting beach crowd

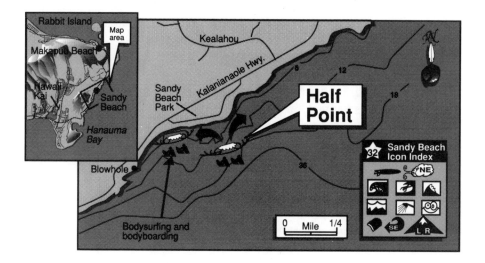

Even the most casual and reluctant reader who finds himself in the unfamiliar terrain of the dictionary will notice that the shortest words frequently have the most complex definitions. The same is true of Sandy Beach. This simple name bring so many other words to mind: pain, pleasure, fear, sun, sand, excitement, power, eternal youth.

In the summertime, Sandys is the ultimate beach hangout in the state, as recently released prisoners of the nation's school system continue their relationships in a more relaxed and enjoyable location. Visitors driving the winding road through the lava fields past Hanauma Bay are mesmerized by the inviting beach at Sandys, and many accept the invitation to snuggle into the warm sand and watch the action in the water.

Many visitors are lured to their doom by the apparent ease with which the island's best bodyboarders and bodysurfers ride these beautiful but deadly waves. People who are barely able to cope with the rigors of a wading pool are suddenly convinced that they can join the young sea gods so gracefully riding these warm turquoise waves. That delusion keeps the lifeguards busier than a one-legged juggler in a butt-kicking contest, as the powerful waves and strong currents drag hapless swimmers into deep water.

Although the waves at Sandy Beach are lovely to gaze upon and break reassuringly close to the beach, they are among the deadliest in the state. Even the most experienced bodysurfers will be tricked into catching a double-suck, triple-jack wave that lures them into the tube of no return and a possible lifetime in a wheelchair.

The wave dredges so much sand that it becomes one of the densest substances in the ocean, compounding the dramatic effect of being slammed into 6 inches of water.

97

Catch one peak as it jacks up, and the bottom of the wave will mutate into its own hollow grinder and the evil twins will treat you to a double-dipper, over-the-falls ride and then squash you into the sand.

It is one of the most deceptively elegant moments in surfing when a bodyboarder casually plugs into a hollow cavern as the lip looms ominously overhead. For one brief instant the world is in harmony, until the whole wave explodes and mauls the bodyboarder.

The main fun zone at Sandy Beach has the best beach and is directly in front of the parking stalls, a fine arrangement that has treated generations to prime views of amazing action in the shorebreak. It's best to arrive early and grab a beachfront parking spot for the entire day.

The middle peak is named Middles, and is flanked by Cobbles and Gas Chambers. If you're really yearning for some excitement, you can match your nerve against Insanities, the spot next to the lava shelf that extends to the Blow Hole. Just remember that enough people have been paralyzed after a headfirst encounter with the sand to staff an impressive wheelchair marathon. During an afternoon of viewing apparent disaster after disaster, you'll come away with a new respect for the resiliency of the human body.

Although there is no law keeping surfers from riding the shorebreak, a higher law prevails in preventing such lunacy. Painful experience has dramatically demonstrated that however glorious the takeoff, it is an ignoble end to be skewered by your board.

However, down the beach toward Makapuu Point, the outside peaks at Generals, Half Point and Full Point are fair game for board surfers. Each summer the visiting professional surfers take over Sandy Beach for a few amazing days. By some unimaginable alchemy, the best surfers in the world paddle out into these woeful, erratic, wind-battered peaks and through the magic of their surfing turn them into astonishing visions of wonder.

Under the spell of these seasoned pros, the same pitiful waves you wouldn't waste your wax on suddenly are transformed into powerful peaks, long walls and tubes.

The area surfers also do a pretty good job of emptying their full bag of tricks on these shifty peaks. It's always a challenge to test your ability against local surfers who have pickled themselves in saltwater while logging the necessary hours to put in a good performance at Sandys.

The waves at Full Point and Half Point feature a confusing mixture of rights and lefts, rights that become lefts and lefts that suddenly turn into rights. The truly adept surfer can make even the most jaded surf observer smile by dropping in on an outside left peak, slamming off an oncoming section and heading right, getting tubed inches away from Devil's Rock, and then doing a 360-degree turn in the shorebreak straight ashore from where he took off.

The best thing about Sandys is that while summer brings the best swells, you can find some sort of wave to enjoy any time of year. With nearly a mile of beachfront, Sandys spreads its arms wide to embrace almost any swell. Sandys will take big east swells, moderate southeast swells and straight south and southwest swells, and turn them into ocean fun.

The wind is generally a sideshore breeze that makes the waves look worse than they really are. And when winds blow from the north or take a vacation, Sandys can provide some mouth-watering tubes.

Although there is plenty of parking all along the coastline here, be careful. Some ambitious thieves make enough money from looting parked cars at Sandys to buy a Third World country. Just make sure that you don't leave anything in your car you won't mind losing.

Back up the beach is a spot called Irma's, just across the street from Kealahou Street, which cuts through the Hawaii Kai Golf Course and heads through Kalama Valley. With a south swell and north wind, Irma's can give you temporary amnesia to make you forget any other spot you've ever surfed. This is part of Wawamalu Beach Park, which doesn't even have a paved parking lot to earn it the status of a park. But the waves more than make up for such a shortcoming.

The beach is a deceptively sandy shore that quickly becomes a deadly maze of coral and lava that have yanked the fins off of many a surfboard. This intimidating bit of coastline is a slack guardian that hasn't kept anybody from surfing these fine waves. Just carefully pick your way through the maze both on the way out and back to the beach, and watch for boils as you ride the waves.

China Walls

Location: Off Koko Kai Beach Park at Portlock Point
Activities: Shortboard surfing, longboard surfing, bodyboarding, sailboarding
Wave: Long performance left, sometimes hollow
Difficulty: Intermediate to advanced surfers
Prime time: April through September
Wave range: All swells with any south, 3-12 feet, straight south is best
Amenities: Parking, legal access to ocean

Long before the first house was built along Portlock Point, the waves at China Walls peeled seemingly as long as the Great Wall in China. Now that the coast and hills of Portlock are covered with mansions, the waves still zip along apparently forever.

It is probably a source of acute distress to the affluent residents of

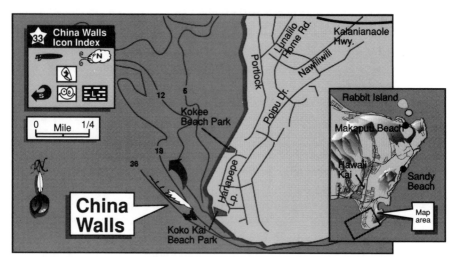

Portlock that the city has placed two tiny parks amid their luxury homes, allowing surfers access to those beckoning waves.

Not that the parks are anything special. It is only by the same generosity of spirit that allows a chihuahua to be called a dog that you can term these weed-infested vacant lots parks. But they do make it easy for surfers to reach the object of their desire.

When a serious summer swell starts battering the spots along the south shore, the surf sites react defensively by closing out. First to go are Waikiki's small-wave sites, followed by the waves that break on the shallow reefs from Hawaii Kai to Black Point. Finally, only a very special few breaks that come alive on only the biggest, baddest swells are left to choose among.

When those swells come booming in, China Walls baits a trap with long, peeling left walls that usually catches the island's most alert surfers. Close your eyes and project on your eyelids your mind's stockpile of footage from Uluwatu in Bali, and you'll be envisioning what China Walls has to offer.

With a special speed-demon board, you can stage a frontside or backside attack on these spinning lefts that will feature every trick you've ever learned. On the absolute choice 10-foot south swell, you will be confronted with the delightful dilemma of how best to catch fire on these long walls. The main question is whether your equipment and ability are enough to keep up with these speeding walls and looping tube sections, and the only way to answer that question is to plug in and shift into overdrive.

But before you vow to start every summer day with a sunrise check of China Walls to make sure these marvelous waves don't slip past you, the depressing truth must be told. Perfect 10- to 12-foot summer swells are as rare as a confirmed sighting of the green flash at sunset, and a 10-foot south swell coupled with benign winds is even more rare.

Luckily, China Walls is a lot of fun even with smaller waves, and will break on most southeast, south and southwest swells. During the smaller swells, the waves break next to an 8-foot ledge at Koko Kai Beach Park that provides access to the waves and a splendid viewing platform for spectators.

It's a quirky sight as well as an odd sensation to ride a wave that breaks close enough to the ledge that you could leap onto the moving peak from land if you were truly daring and nimble. When the waves are bigger, entering the water by leaping from the ledge produces a few tense moments, but nothing compared to the nerve-frazzling tactic of letting a wave surge carry you high enough to scale the ledge after you've finished your session.

Not all surfers possess the delicate timing and agility necessary for such a maneuver, and many have been hurt in the attempt. If you are too drained from hours of surfing or are daunted by the swells crashing on the cliff, just head down the shore about 100 yards to Kokee Beach Park, where the land meets the sea in a much less dramatic manner.

The Koolau Mountains and the back side of Koko Crater funnel the trade winds straight into waves at China Walls. This blessing/curse makes even sideshore winds blow offshore, but also increases the speed of the wind. While this makes paddling for waves difficult, it also holds up the walls and makes them break hollower.

Getting to China Walls is complicated by the labyrinth of streets in Portlock, all named after places on Kauai. Just turn off Kalanianaole Highway at Lunalilo Home Road, across from the Koko Marina Shopping Center, and follow it until you reach Poipu Drive. Turn left and then right on Poipu Drive until it intersects Hanapepe Loop, which will lead you to both Kokee Place, site of Kokee Beach Park, and Hanapepe Place, site of Koko Kai Beach Park. You can park on the cul de sac at either place long enough to check the waves, but if you're going to surf you'll have to park along Hanapepe Loop and walk back down to either park.

While Koko Kai Park is closer to the waves, Kokee Park provides a better straight-on view of the surf action. At Koko Kai you have the thrill of watching surfers ripping the waves at your feet, but you're forced to watch from behind as the surfers ride away from you.

The best way to reach the lineup at China Walls is to just follow one of the trails down to the ledge at Koko Kai Park, and time your leap into the ocean to coincide with the arrival of a wave. It's rather bad form as well as intensely painful to start your surf session by leaping when the wave recedes and landing on bare coral. The locals will figure you for a hopeless twit and never give you a wave.

The waves here break along the eastern edge of gigantic Maunalua Bay, which creates some fierce currents as water rushes out to sea. It's not much of a problem on smaller days, but when the waves are big a brutish set can snatch sunbathers, spectators and fishermen from their vantage point on the ledge and sweep them into the ocean, where the dreaded Molokai Express current can take them far from shore.

It's kind of spooky surfing out here at land's end, bobbing around in the kind of deep-blue water that surely must be spawning ground for belly-slashing sea monsters. When you gaze out to sea for an approaching set, the next small chunk of land is Tahiti, thousands of miles away.

Paddling back out to the lineup after a ride on a fun day of waves is simple: just keep duck-diving as each wave breaks, and although you will be swept toward the middle of the bay, eventually you will reach the channel or the end of the set. On a bigger day, you can either end your wave with a flyaway kickout and hit the water in mid-stroke, or wipe out and brace yourself for a hellish pounding as the rest of the set pushes you over to the distant channel. Don't despair, eventually the set will end or deep water will rescue you, and you can catch your breath as you slowly paddle back out to the lineup beyond the breaking waves.

Because the winds blow so fiercely here, you'll find the cleanest conditions during early morning and late afternoon, or on windless or north wind days.

Smaller days will allow you to perfect your slashing technique on lefts, but if you luck into one of those coveted double-overhead days, you'll have saved thousands of dollars and enjoyed just as exciting a session as the blokes who opted for a trip to Bali.

The takeoff at China Walls is so close to the cliff that spectators can pass you a drink. But the end of the line is far, far away. Photo: Warren Bolster.

CHAPTER 2

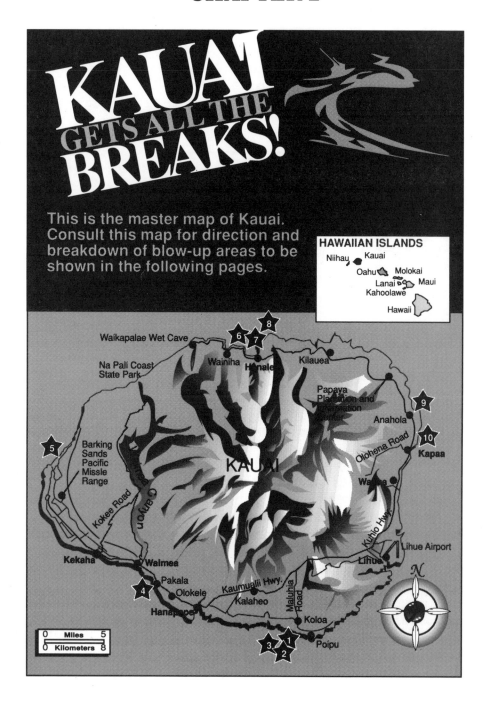

KAUAI
GETS ALL THE
BREAKS!

This is the master map of Kauai. Consult this map for direction and breakdown of blow-up areas to be shown in the following pages.

HAWAIIAN ISLANDS

Niihau   Kauai
Oahu   Molokai
Lanai   Maui
Kahoolawe

Hawaii

Longhouse

Location: Off of sea wall fronting Beach House restaurant
Activities: Shortboard surfing, longboard surfing, bodyboarding
Wave: Fast hollow left, rebreak rights
Difficulty: Intermediate to expert surfers
Prime time: April through September
Wave range: All swells with any south, 2-8 feet, southeast is best
Amenities: Parking, showers, restrooms, excellent viewing area

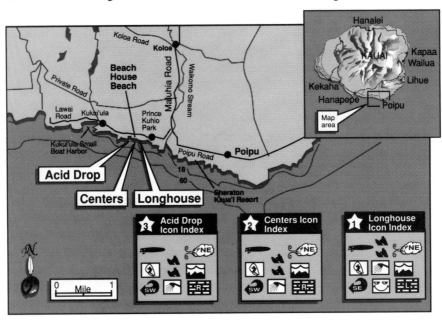

If you lead a truly good life and aren't reincarnated as a dolphin or sea otter, then perhaps you will spend Eternity lounging on the lawn beside the Beach House restaurant in Poipu.

From this supreme vantage point, on a southwest or south swell you are looking right into the gaping jaws of waves at Acid Drop and Centers. And during a southeast swell, a strategic seat on the nearby sea wall will let you watch as surfers shred the lefts at Longhouse, one of the premiere lefts in the state.

If you are entertaining any notions about showing the Kauai boys how to rip, be warned: these guys can take a fearsome, pitching peak and turn it upside down and inside out with their amazing antics.

Some of the more adept Kauai surfers can catch a snarling, jacking 8-foot left at Longhouse and make the drop with only a moist inside rail holding them in, then jam a last-second turn as the lip misses decapitating them by inches and fly along a speeding wall that always seems on the verge of ripping them off their board. They will then stall into an inside-out barrel, casually emerge and do a floater on the closeout inside section.

All of this takes place within yards of the best viewing spots along the edge of the seawall, which puts you right on the waves with the surfers.

Longtime residents call the spot Longhouse after the Tahitian Longhouse restaurant that originally occupied this choice site. Other surfers call it PKs, for Prince Kuhio Park on the beach, which provides welcome parking, showers and restrooms.

But the main hangout is the lawn and seawall in front of the Beach House, where a gracious restaurant management provides access to the surf and lets weary surfers and mesmerized spectators lounge and enjoy the show. During the late spring, summer and early fall months, patrons of the Beach House are treated to a dazzling display of surf action as south and southwest swells cause Acid Drop and Centers to fire, while southeast swells bring Longhouse to life.

Shortboarders, longboarders and bodyboarders all heed the call of the long, winding, hollow lefts of Longhouse, but only the very best do well here. The wave begins with a steep drop that can make you gag with vertigo, and the lip is quick to pitch out and swat slow or timid surfers. The wave quickly continues its aggressive attempt to rid itself of irksome riders as it winds down the reef at a frightening pace.

After a few meaningful encounters with the reef, a sense of urgency will begin to guide your moves until you begin to match the waves' blinding velocity. At that point you'll realize why this spot is always packed with contenders whenever the southeast swell is caressed by a northeast wind.

To reach Longhouse, take Kaumualii Highway until it intersects Maluhia Road, and follow that until you reach Lawai Road. If you turn left onto Poipu Road you will be lost forever, so just remember right is right. The road will eventually take you to a memorable sight: three great surf spots in a row, easily visible from the road.

Just because you are on an Outer Island, don't expect to be forced to surf these waves alone. The Poipu area is a hot development property, and there is a large population of recent transplants who have swelled the ranks of local surfers to a depressing number.

Don't let the crowds paralyze you into staying on the beach. Get out there and see if you can't snatch a few choice waves with your ability and cunning.

Parking is no problem, with a paved lot at Prince Kuhio Park and spots along the beachfront on Lawai Road. Access to the waves at Longhouse is simple as well. Just walk along the seawall beside the Beach House, clamber down the rocks in front and start stroking for the gap where the lefts of Longhouse and the rights of Centers meet.

With good timing, a little luck and some determined paddling you'll shoot the gap and be in the lineup within minutes. With a little bad luck or laggard paddling the waves will wrench your board out of your death grip and bonk you with it.

Another favorite trick the waves use on unsuspecting surfers is to suck the thin covering of water off the rocks and coral heads and impale your surfboard while you're paddling for your life. Caution is essential when paddling out here.

On the inside section the confused mass of white water will magically form into a fun little right that is the delight of younger surfers and bodyboarders, and lets them ride right up to the rocks along the point.

It is a moment of exquisite stylishness for a surfer on the outside to get barreled upon takeoff and emerge at the end of the wave, bounce off the closeout section, work the rebreak right and casually step off his board onto the seawall. This is guaranteed to drive even the most oblivious tourist guzzling mai tais at the Beach House bar into a frenzy of appreciation.

The waves at Longhouse will take a variety of south swells, but a solid southwest swell will turn it into a horrid mass of white water. When the waves hit 3 to 4 feet, they are playful and forgiving. As they increase in size they become more menacing, and when they get much over 8 feet you won't want to have anything to do with them, as the reef and channel just can't cope with that much energy.

While easterly trade winds are side offshore, more northerly trades are straight offshore, and glassy mornings and evenings do a wonderful bit of cosmetic surgery on these long walls.

And after a hard day of plugging into the barrel and grappling with the tube monster, you can always secure a strategic table at the Beach House and inhale Zombies until the whole day is painted with a gilded glow as you watch surfers terrorizing the waves you recently abandoned.

Centers

Location: Between Longhouse and Acid Drop off Prince Kuhio Beach Park
Activities: Shortboard surfing, longboard surfing, bodyboarding
Wave: Fast hollow right, some lefts
Difficulty: Intermediate to expert surfers
Prime time: April through September
Wave range: All swells with any south, 2-8 feet, southwest is best
Amenities: Beachfront parking, showers, restroom

If you just can't cope with the overwhelming drop and tube at Acid Drop, you can just paddle up the reef to Centers, which on an overhead day is merely frightening where Acid Drop is terrifying.

Centers, cunningly named for its location between two prime surf spots, features the same dizzying elevator takeoff as Acid Drop and a similar if less punishing cylinder. Of course, the wave ends in the same dreaded exposed rocks and shallow reef on the inside section.

It is probably of scant comfort that a wipeout at Centers will only maim you, while the wave at Acid Drop will attempt to kill you. But that small distinction is enough to give surfers an alternative when Acid Drop is in an especially ugly mood.

With an overhead south swell and northerly winds, the wave at Centers jacks up and pitches in a shrieking tube that will inspire a howl of elation when you emerge from the barrel. The wall at Centers is a bit more tapered than the slamming closeout that often greets surfers exiting the tube at Acid Drop, which is a splendid feature that almost everyone appreciates.

The crowd at Centers is also quite a bit less intense than the tube mongers that dominate at Acid Drop, as it is mostly made up of surfers who were intimidated by the aggressive energy level of the crowd at Acid Drop and weary of being cuffed around by the waves.

Don't be surprised at the number of bodyboarders that entrust their safety to their fragile slivers of plastic foam as they free-fall down the steep wave faces and gamely plug into improbable barrels. They will frequently astound you by pulling off maneuvers that surfers don't even dream of.

The best way to reach the lineup is to park in a strategic spot along Lawai Road and paddle out from the rock-lined beach. There is a slight gap between the rights at Acid Drop and the lefts at Centers, but you'll have to slip past the vigilant guardian rocks and coral heads with care. If your timing is right you can hit it between sets and reach the lineup with dry hair. With a little bad luck the biggest set of the day will unload on your head and do its best to wrest your board from your steel grasp and beat you over the head with it.

Don't panic, just keep duck-diving and hold your position, and eventually even the most evil set will end and you can make it to deeper water. This tactic also works after a wipeout, or at the end of a ride when the next few waves in the set close out.

By some arcane mystery of offshore topography and little-understood principles of oceanography, a 5-foot swell on Oahu is magically transformed into a 7-foot swell on Kauai. So when you're sitting out at Centers, resting between trips to the tube, you can be forgiven if you smirk at the thought of the surfers in Honolulu forced to endure smaller waves and bigger crowds.

When the swell comes in from the southeast, the lefts get better than the rights and can be a lot of fun, though less hollow than the rights on a good day. With a solid southwest swell, the rights will line up and wind down the line forever, treating you to a session that will drive your friends mad with envy whenever you tell the tale.

Acid Drop

Location: Fronting Prince Kuhio Beach Park, Poipu
Activities: Shortboard surfing, longboard surfing, bodyboarding
Wave: Ultra-hollow, short right
Difficulty: Experts only
Prime time: Best April through September
Wave range: All swells with any south, 2-12 feet, southwest is best
Amenities: Parking, showers, restroom, wonderful view from the beach

Acid Drop is dramatic proof that you don't need to take drugs for a mind-altering experience. Given its whimsical name by playful surfers during the drug-dazed '60s, the waves at Acid Drop are a trip and a half and guaranteed to blow your mind. Waves journey thousands of miles through the South Pacific and receive a rude greeting when they slam into the shallow reef at Acid Drop. They leap up in protest and pitch forward, and woe to anyone they get ahold of.

If you are adept and have unshakable faith in your board and your ability, you can stroke into the most insane drop on a jacking peak, hold your edge and ease into a liquid cavern as the lip pitches over. If the tube monster is feeling generous, you will emerge howling from the pit. Otherwise, when the whip comes down you will be slammed onto a nightmarish Venusian seascape of a reef. Pain is more than probable; it's promised.

To make the situation more challenging, there is no channel at Acid Drop, no zone of safety to retreat to when caught inside or to aim for when in the tube. While some waves will provide a closed-out section to greet your emergence from the barrel, others will taper to a reassuringly delicate shoulder. When you're stroking frantically to catch one of these double-jacking peaks, you always try to convince yourself you are heading for one of the finely tapered walls and not the horrendous hammer.

Depending on how your last wave ended, you will vow that it is worth any punishment to experience the rush of the drop and thrill of the tube at Acid Drop, and most tube junkies will give their impassioned agreement. But while your body can heal itself, you better have a large quiver of boards if you intend to challenge Acid Drop. This spot is an uncultured brute that will snap your board as a snack and use the jagged fiberglass edges to pick the teeth of the reef on the inside section.

Getting out to the waves at Acid Drop is tricky, but easier than deciding whether you are up for the adventure that awaits you in the lineup. You can check the waves from Lawai Road, which fronts the beach and provides an excellent view of the wave action. With a little luck you can find a choice roadside parking spot and choose just the right music on your car sound system to help you make the important decision about whether to paddle out.

The shoreline is rocky and the paddle to the lineup is shallow and mined with coral heads that loom unexpectedly, so use caution. The peak is guarded by a ring of exposed rocks, and there is no channel, so time the sets with precision and stroke like crazy immediately after the largest wave of the set has broken. With luck, there will be a sufficient lull between sets to let you make your way out to the waves. If not, some adroit duck-diving should get you through any surprise sets.

When you take the inevitable wipeout, try to use your feet as a buffer to keep the more important portions of your anatomy off the reef. Let the white water carry you over toward the shoulder while the rest of the set breaks.

Some surfers are reduced to gibbering fools when they make a filthy wave here, while others are reduced to tears by a dreadful pounding, but everyone is usually dramatically affected by taking a perfectly legal trip at Acid Drop.

Pakalas

Location: West of Hanapepe, before Waimea
Activities: Shortboard surfing, longboard surfing, bodyboarding
Wave: Fast performance left, often hollow
Difficulty: Intermediate to expert surfers
Prime time: Best April through September, breaks all year
Wave range: All swells with any south, 3-10 feet, south-southeast is best
Amenities: Parking, relaxing hike

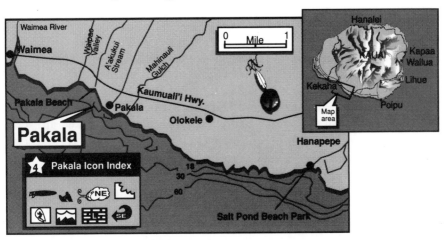

There are those special surf spots whose waves are so doleful that surfers can barely juice themselves up to walk 10 feet from the parking lot and paddle out. Then you have the magical surf sites where surfers will crawl five

KAUAI GETS ALL THE BREAKS!

Pakala's question
The question? Will you survive? Outer island picturesque and dangerous. What do you want? Paradise?

Far Point

Middles

Bowl

BEWARE!
Shallow sharp reef

BEWARE!
Coral heads

Pakala Village

1/4 mile

Paddle out 75 yards

Groin

Pakalas:
This break is best at 8 feet and under on a Southeast swell and North winds. You can expect hollow rippable walls, but watch out for the coral heads and sharks.

miles over broken glass and paddle through shark-infested water just to sample the waves.

The latter is the case with Pakalas, one of the aquatic treasures of the Hawaiian Islands. Back in the '60s and '70s surfers either hiked two miles from Waimea along a rugged coast or took a shortcut and risked arrest by policemen acting on behalf of protective landowners. But Pakalas is the kind of hormone-stimulating wave that inspires such devotion.

Kauai County has taken the trauma from reaching Pakalas, providing access by a short hike on an easy trail. Amazingly, despite the easy access these alluring waves are frequently uncrowded.

Pakalas is also called Infinities, a name you'll comprehend the moment you plug into one of these screaming, fast walls and find yourself blazing along the track to eternity. South swells hit the reef fronting the village at Pakala Point and start spinning down the reef until they hit the deep water of Hoanuanu Bay a few hundred yards later.

Hop onto one of these speedsters and along the way you will hit speeds fast enough to melt the resin off your board and leave the fiberglass intact as you fly from filthy barrel to nasty section, pausing only long enough to see how deeply you can get tubed and still make the wave.

After a good day at Infinities you'll brainstorm for any implausible scheme to raise the cash to purchase a piece of property nearby. Failing that, you'll commit every waking second on Kauai to planning another session here, and wonder why anyone would ever want to surf anywhere else.

There are a few drawbacks to surfing Pakalas, however. The reef that makes these waves peel so perfectly and break so hollow is a sharp battleground seemingly designed by a malevolent creator intent on testing how much abuse surfers will endure for good waves.

At low tide, a wipeout will put you right on top of this reef and will provide hours of painful entertainment later as you attempt to identify the fascinating variety of sea organisms you are extracting from your body. You should try to land feet first during a wipeout to keep more sensitive parts of your body free from agonizing intrusion.

Straightening out at low tide is to be reserved for moments of pure desperation, as you will likely lose your fins and possibly a few fingers. Duck-diving at low tide on the shallow reef flat is not only not recommended, it's not possible. There just isn't enough water between the wave and the reef to accommodate you and your board. Far better to stand on the coral and leap into the oncoming wave until you hit deeper water.

Just around the corner to the east is a stream whose sole function seems to be discharging an impressive volume of silt to make the waves look like undulating liquid chocolate. This is great camouflage for sharks, and sightings are common.

But these problems are mere trifles when considering the delights that Pakalas has to offer. On a merely average day, the wave will divide into three distinct peaks, each offering a 75-yard or longer ride and multiple visits to the tube. The most crowded peak is usually the one closest to the bay, as it offers an easy paddle back out through the deep water at the edge of the reef.

It's an easy matter to ditch the crowd by heading for the less packed peaks toward the point.

At higher tide the tubes are less frequent, but the sections become more makable and you can whip out floaters, lip bashes and whitewater rebounds without fearing the reef's fangs.

When everything comes together, the waves line up for a 300-yard speed run that will turn your legs to jelly and leave your spirit soaring and eager for another dose. Long after your arms are limp from the long paddle back out to the lineup you'll be painfully dragging yourself along for another hit of pleasure.

Way out at the point, bobbing in the giant vat of liquid chocolate, if you gaze back toward Hanapepe you will see empty waves peeling toward you, and on the palm-studded beach a few simple houses. Surrender, and your imagination will convince you that you are on an exotic surf trip in a remote corner of the world.

As you pass through Hanapepe heading west, keep an eye on your car's odometer, and at about three miles keep a sharp lookout for a short bridge, with cars parked on each side of the street just west of the bridge. Add your car to the lot and locate the trailhead just beside the bridge. Follow it to a stream, and if this is to be your lucky day, offshore on the other side of the stream will be some of the finest lefts imaginable.

The water beside the breakwater is shallow, with coral heads lurking in the murky water, and many people take the longer paddle on the other side of the jetty in deeper water as they head for the waves. Just pick the peak that suits your fancy, and have fun.

The best way to reach the beach is to surf your way to the inside peak near the jetty, catch one wave as far as you can ride it and head for the deeper water until you hit the shore.

The trade winds are offshore here, making the already hollow waves even rounder. Windless mornings are a real treat, and only kona winds or sea breezes will give these dreamy waves a nightmarish aspect.

Polihale

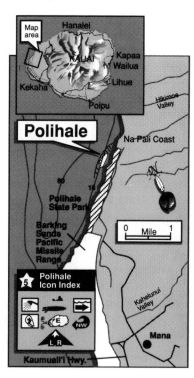

Location: Along Polihale State Park
Activities: Shortboard surfing, longboard surfing, bodyboarding, bodysurfing, sailboarding
Wave: Powerful beachbreak peaks, sometimes hollow, some reef breaks
Difficulty: Beginning to expert surfers
Prime time: Best September through April, breaks all year
Wave range: All swells with any west, 2-8 feet, west-northwest is best
Amenities: Parking, camping, showers, restrooms, miles of empty beach

When you reach the end of the road at Polihale and stand on the shore looking southwest, you are facing 15 miles of sandy beach. Although it would be a daunting task to trudge those 15 miles on foot, along the way you would find enough good surf spots to keep you amused for the next 15 years. Because of Kauai's rounded contours, winter and summer swells wrap around the coast and provide year-round wave action on the west shore.

It is also a gracious gift of nature that the winds on this side are usually offshore or absent, which makes the waves a pure delight until the occasional malevolent kona winds blow onshore.

This stretch of coastline is dangerous even during the summer. Don't be seduced into a false sense of safety by the friendly blue sky and the lovely turquoise water. The bottom drops off quickly here, and the currents will pull you into deep water and keep you from reaching the beach before you know you're in trouble. When you're out surfing just be alert, find some permanent features on the beach to line up with, and constantly check your lineups.

During the summer the waves adopt a gentle manner, and provide the kind of quick peaks and hollow sections that beginners and more experienced surfers can enjoy with equal appreciation.

Come back during the winter, and you won't believe you're at the same place. The bigger northwest swells break much farther from the warm, wide sandy beach, and the currents can drag you off to Niihau before you even realize you are moving. The same friendly peaks that were so playful during the summer are now ill-tempered beasts more likely to swat you aside than let you finish your ride. Because the waves break over sandbars, the peaks shift from place to place, and will drive you mad by peeling perfectly just beyond your grasp. And when you paddle over to where the last wave broke so invitingly, the next wave will peel mockingly from the spot you just vacated.

Still, when you do snag one of these board-snapping barrels you'll forget your own name in your haste to paddle out for another fix.

The lineup depends on what kind of mood the sandbar is in that day, but with miles of beach to choose from, you can usually find a peak that is going off. And if other surfers begin to cluster around you, it's a simple matter to stroke over to the next peak for a little isolation.

From 3-6 feet these waves will let you perfect any improbable maneuver that you've ever seen anyone else attempt. Conditions become progressively more limiting and dangerous as the waves get bigger, until at 10 feet and bigger the whole area is buried under a seething mass of white water. Although there are still ridable waves at that size, the currents are so potent and the lineup so difficult to reach that most people leave Polihale alone and head for reefs that can handle the size.

To get to this promised sand, follow Kaumualii Highway toward Mana, then turn left through the cane fields and follow the signs toward Polihale State Park. Soon you will be confronted with a dilemma: do you follow the road to the end of the line and begin searching for the best wave, or do you start veering left off the road to the enticing side trails to check the reefs and sandbars along the way until you reach road's end?

Either way your preference for a particular type of wave will determine which spot will be favored with your performance that day. If you were really ambitious and energetic, you could sample the entire spectrum of waves along the coast in one day, paddling and driving from peak to peak. Of course, it might take you a week to recharge your batteries after such an odyssey.

The surf here breaks on a lonely shore far from civilization, so it's a good idea to fill your cooler in Waimea or Kekaha with savory items so you won't have to cut your surf patrol short in a frantic mission to find food.

Waikoko

Location: West side of Hanalei Bay
Activities: Shortboard surfing, longboard surfing, bodyboarding
Wave: Fast performance left, often hollow
Difficulty: Intermediate to expert surfers
Prime time: September through April
Wave range: All swells with any north, 2-15 feet, north-northwest is best
Amenities: Parking along Kuhio Highway, splendid beach, exotic scenery

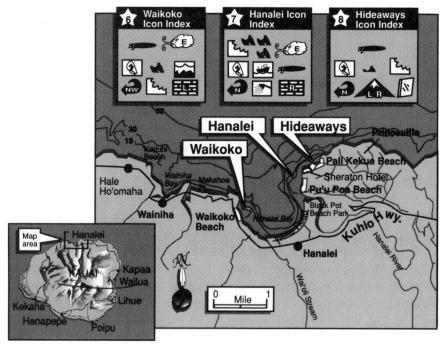

Embraced by the protective arms of Hanalei Bay is a wonderland of surf spots, starting with Waikoko on the west side of the bay.

Attempting to surf Waikoko when conditions are wrong isn't worth the world of pain and misery that awaits you, as the shallow reef, fierce currents and sea urchins will join the snarling waves in punishing you for your poor judgment.

While Hanalei Point on the east side of the bay is somewhat protected by the cliffs from the trade winds, Waikoko is naked to the torment of the trades and is often plagued by cross chop that builds up as the wind shrieks across the expanse of water that fills the bay.

But when a solid north-northeast swell is soothed by gentle east winds, the hollow lefts that come grinding along Waikoko Reef are worth any suffering the coral might inflict.

When the wind forgets to blow and a glassy blanket spreads over the ocean, the waves at Waikoko are silken smooth humps that pitch and peel when they hit the reef. Then anything is possible, and your performance will be limited only by your imagination.

On smaller days, Waikoko's winding lefts are a bodyboarder's delight, and will provide long rippable walls and hollow sections. As the waves get bigger, the potential for disaster increases, and by the time the waves top double overhead, many surfers pause a long time on the beach weighing their chances against these ill-humored bushwhackers.

Armed with the right board, a reckless disregard for personal safety and heaps of ability, Waikoko will take you to the edge of fear and push you right over the brink into exhilaration. But you really have to force yourself to stroke convincingly for these waves as they come sweeping around the point and wailing down the reef on a search-and-destroy mission with you as the target. Any hint of hesitation and these waves will pitch you with the lip and deliver a good old-fashioned stomping.

Waikoko Reef absorbs the bulk of the surf's energy and renders it harmless, so families can enjoy the relative safety of the water near the shore. Surfers grabbing the waves that peel along the reef's outer edge often absorb quite a bit of that energy when they wipe out. And if the reef bounce doesn't uphold Waikoko's high standards of pain, the vast herds of sea urchins are always ready to perform a little acupuncture to boost the pain level.

As you reach the west end of Hanalei Bay and Kuhio Highway starts to climb toward Lumahai Beach, you'll have one last quick glimpse of the ocean. If you see lefts peeling along the reef, slam on the brakes and screech to the side of the road, then sprint down one of the trails to the beach, board tucked securely under your arm. You are in for a wonderful session.

Attempting to punch through the waves in a straight-on assault to reach the lineup is fairly worthless, and a good way to earn a body slam onto the reef. Far better to spare yourself the abuse by paddling around the end section of the waves after they have lost some of their fury, and paddle back toward the point where the waves begin their kamikaze run along the reef edge.

After the inevitable wipeout, after the waves have ceased working you over, you might gaze at the long paddle around the end section of the reef with dismay and try to dupe yourself into attempting the shorter paddle straight back out. That might work on smaller days, but when the waves are overhead they make great sport of cruelly crushing surfers a few strokes short of making it back to the lineup.

Most surfers are reluctant to subject themselves to such abuse, but those who accept Waikoko's challenge are rewarded with wailing left walls spiced with hollow sections. And that is worth any risk.

Hanalei Point

Location: East side of Hanalei Bay
Activities: Shortboard surfing, longboard surfing, sailboarding, bodyboarding
Wave: Ultimate fast, long performance right, often hollow
Difficulty: Beginning to expert surfers
Prime time: September through April
Wave range: All swells with any north, 3-20 feet, north is best
Amenities: Parking, showers, restrooms, picnic tables, shelters

In 1973 Kauai County opened to the public one of the great beach parks of the world. Although modest by almost any standard, with restrooms, showers, a small parking lot and a few picnic tables, Black Pot Beach Park gives surfers unrestricted access to Kauai's greatest ocean resource: the perfect peaks of Hanalei Point.

Named after the communal black cooking pot used by locals who gathered in the area before the park was created, the beach park is the staging area for expeditions launched to conquer Hanalei's endless waves.

Your first glimpse of the waves at Hanalei is likely to be a religious experience. This wave is a fierce competitor for the title of the state's best right. If another surf spot seeks to steal your vote by showing you a good time, Hanalei will flaunt its heaviest, longest lines and dare you to ride them. And if you accept that challenge, you'll paddle back out like a maniac after the first blazing wall, howling with desire for another dose and convinced that Hanalei is the best righthander in the universe.

Hanalei boasts three takeoff spots that each provide all the thrills most mortals can handle. But on those special occasions when all three connect, it's an overdose of pleasure that can threaten your sanity.

The outside peak is called Impossibles, a descriptive title that doesn't discourage anyone from trying to cope with the steep drop and generate enough speed to make the quick, hollow sections. If you can connect all the dots, or your board has the unholy propulsion properties of a Ferrari F-40, you will fly at full steam into the immensely hollow Flat Rock section. With a little luck and a lot of speed, your down-the-line tour will bring you to the final trip to the tube at the Bowl, the end of the line.

When the waves at Hanalei are in a playful mood and waist high to slightly overhead, you can string together any wild combination of maneuvers to punctuate your visits to the tube. Tube rides are a yawningly common sight here, but emerging from the tube with enough speed and style to make subsequent sections will turn heads every time.

The waves become more exciting as they get bigger, and by the time they are double overhead the waves start glowering and sessions become harrowing. Because the reef is so shallow, the current rushes parallel to the waves and drags surfers over to the channel. It's possible to punch straight through back to the lineup on smaller days and between sets, but when it gets really big most surfers let the rip carry them to the channel and make the long paddle back to the lineup.

Some surfers impulsively take a chance and try to windmill it straight back out even on bigger days, and when it works, it's a great shortcut. However, if one of these hostile waves squeezes you, there is no way you'll get all that toothpaste back into your tube.

When you paddle for one of the outside peaks, you have to keep your eyes down the line, focus all your attention down the line, catch the wave at an angle and hit your turn halfway down the wave face. If you fool around, by the time you reach the bottom of the wave to hit your turn you'll look up and see you're too late to hop the freight train thundering down the tracks.

As the most northerly of the main Hawaiian Islands, Kauai is the first obstacle winter waves encounter. This means that Kauai surfers score each swell first and biggest, and that Kauai takes the brunt of each cold front that comes sweeping through. Frequently the rain clouds and howling winds exhaust themselves in tormenting Kauai and spare the rest of the islands.

This assault by heavy weather plays havoc with the conditions at Hanalei Bay, where many fine swells are destroyed by stormy conditions. But then will come days when the clouds have vanished and the winds have overslept, leaving blue skies and glassy waves. Those are days to live for.

East winds will also brush the blemishes from Hanalei's waves, and will help hold the tube open longer to increase your chances of a safe exit.

To find Hanalei Point, turn off Kuhio Highway on any road in Hanalei town, then turn right on Weke Road and follow it until you reach the Hanalei Pier and nearby Black Pot Beach Park.

The easiest way to reach the lineup is to leave your car at Black Pot Beach Park and start stroking out, veering slightly to the right. At low tide you'll have to wade across the sandbar before the river, and while crossing the river don't give the boaters an easy target for their propellers.

Keep heading for the deep channel at the end of the Bowl; once you've turned the corner it's time to start foraging. Many people prefer the pleasures of the Bowl, with the safety of the channel so comfortingly close. While the Bowl will provide all the thrills you can handle, with a steep takeoff and long hollow section, the other peaks will continually beckon.

One fun strategy is to rove among the three peaks, sampling the delights of each and hoping for those special waves that let you test your full-blast capacity to make the full uninterrupted streak from point to bowl.

Although sharks are sporadically active in Hanalei Bay, the vast throngs of surfers increase the odds that someone else will be the victim. A depressingly large and vigorous community of surfers in Hanalei ensures that you will never know the joy of surfing these waves alone. The most you can hope for is to snatch an occasional session between peak crowds. But you'll soon find that one wave at Hanalei is worth a half dozen almost anywhere else.

Hideaways

Location: Beneath the cliffs at Princeville
Activities: Shortboard surfing, longboard surfing, bodyboarding
Wave: Performance right and left peak, sometimes hollow
Difficulty: Beginning to expert surfers
Prime time: September through May
Wave range: All swells with any north, 2-6 feet
Amenities: Parking, wonderful beach, great scenery

You've spent nearly a week doing the daily dawn check because you're fiending for some of those mythical, peeling rights of Hanalei Point, only to be mocked by tiny, wind-lashed waves. But today is different. The waves are still limp, mutant dwarves, but this morning is glassy, and you're still fiending for waves.

It's time to take a side trip to adventure. Follow the road to Princeville, and a quick but treacherous hike down a cliff will bring you to a nifty little tropical treat called Hideaways. This bitty pocket of sand snuggled up against a lushly landscaped cliff is one of Hawaii's tiny treasures, and one of the best reasons for venturing away from the more famous surf spots.

As you emerge from the trail you will see a secluded beach framed by exotic foliage with wonderfully translucent blue water offshore. If the wind is on vacation and the waves pay a visit, you will be rewarded with a relaxing surf session in playful performance waves.

Because it sits exposed on the open ocean, Hideaways is usually bullied by the trade winds. But when the kona winds blow or on those special glassy mornings, the waves become Kauai's goodwill ambassadors, eager to show you a good time.

Up to 6 feet, the waves peak up on a small reef and peel right and left, allowing you to surf yourself silly frontside and then shift gears to perfect your backside attack. When the swell grows impatient with fooling around and gets serious, the waves overpower the reef and blow the little beach away as whitewater washes up and rebounds off the cliff. But you don't care, you'll be off grappling with the crowd at Hanalei anyway.

The wonderful isolation of Hideaways is both a curse and a blessing. It's a delirious treat to surf fun waves in Hawaii with only a few surfers to share them with, but between sets you might find yourself thinking about how it might be better if the sharks had a few other people to choose among when they make their meal selection.

Although shark attacks are rare, it's somewhat depressing to contemplate scaling the cliff after your appendages have been mauled. Still, the next set will drive those distressing thoughts away as you select the choicest wave of the set.

To get to this little slice of paradise, turn off Kuhio Highway at the entrance to Princeville and follow the signs to the Sheraton Princeville Hotel. Turn into the first hotel parking lot, walk to the cliff-top edge of the lot and try to keep your friends from howling with laughter as you descend the steep, slippery steps while balancing your surfboard and other equipment.

A decrepit handrail will help you balance as you follow the trail through the dense foliage to the sandy beach. Before you surf yourself to exhaustion, remember to save enough strength to make your way back up the cliff.

You may have to search harder to find them these days, but there are still places where you can be alone with your thoughts. Photo: Mike Tsukamoto

Unreals

Location: South end of Anahola Bay, north of Kapaa
Activities: Shortboard surfing, longboard surfing, bodyboarding
Wave: Fast performance right, often hollow
Difficulty: Beginning to expert surfers
Prime time: Breaks all year
Wave range: All swells with any east, 2-8 feet
Amenities: Parking, wonderful beach, great scenery

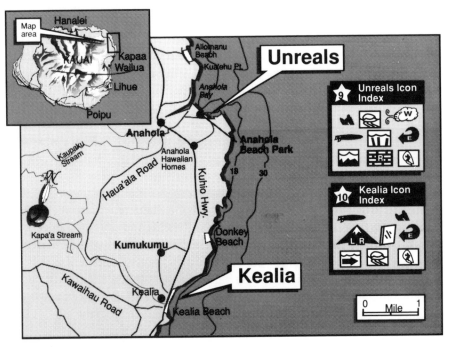

When you grow weary of jousting with the crowds that infest most of Kauai's famous surf spots, it's time to start searching for more anonymous spots where you can find a few waves to yourself.

After being hassled for every wave that hits the reef by a seemingly endless supply of wave hogs, that razor edge of excitement begins to dull as you start to doubt your ability. Take your troubled spirit to Anahola Bay, where a good solo session at Unreals will restore your faith in yourself and renew your addiction to surfing.

Although the trade winds frequently blow out the east shore's exposed spots, Unreals is nestled under the protective bulk of Kahala Point and escapes some of the wind's ravages.

Glassy mornings and kona winds will smooth the bumps off these waves and leave in their place fine-textured walls that beg you to carve petroglyphs on them with your surfboard.

120

Large north-northwest swells wrap into the bay and bring delectable right peaks and long walls, as do smaller north and northeast swells. The most generous wave-bringers are the east swells, which funnel straight into the bay. Add kona winds to an east swell and you'll end up with waves that will quickly erase any distasteful memory of ravening crowds.

Unreals is playful from 3-5 feet, but when the swell bulks up, the lineup changes and the wave assumes a menacing aspect that earns the spot the name Gas Chambers. The name is more appropriate than most, as the shallow reef and harsh currents can create a terminal situation for unwary surfers.

If you're cruising Kuhio Highway from the north, turn left on Hauaala Road just after you cross the bridge over the Anahola River. Follow the road until it branches to the right, and watch for a series of short dirt roads on the left that lead to the ocean. Any one of them will take you to the waves.

While the surrounding forest is picturesque, it also provides perfect cover for thieves, so hide your car key. If a lapse of consciousness has resulted in the unwanted presence of items you're still fond of, carry them up the beach with you and leave them in plain sight of the lineup. That may not keep anyone from stealing them, but if you get to watch the thieves in action at least you won't be expecting to find the items when you return to your car.

You'll have an easier time spotting Unreals than reaching the lineup. Once you spot the protruding remnants of an abandoned landing, look to the right. If you are destined to surf that day you'll spot an unmistakable sign: an exquisite right peeling toward you. Just don't forget that these waves are guarded by a vicious reef that is always eager to taste new meat. Watch where the wave ends, and gingerly stroke over the reef until you hit deeper water; then paddle just outside the break and head for the takeoff spot.

The waves hit the shallow reef with gut-wrenching abruptness, so be prepared to act quickly when you spot a desirable wave, or you'll have plenty of time to lament your slowness as you take the free-fall and double spin cycle over the falls.

When all the elements come together, Unreals is a high-performance wave blessed with spinning cylinders and lips just begging to be bashed. Some frantic surfers are able to cram a late drop, power turn, lip bash, whitewater bounce cutback, tube ride and floater into one frenzied sequence on a wave, but almost anyone is able to whip out any three of those maneuvers per wave.

As you dismantle these waves, just remember to kick out before you impale yourself on the pilings of the old landing, which would be a spectacular if gruesome way to end a ride.

It will also save you a lot of grief to paddle away from the old pier quickly when caught inside, as the white water can make a game of seeing how far you'll bounce when it slams you into the pilings.

This area is a perfect setting for a picnic when the waves aren't any good, and you can spend an entire day beachwalking, swimming, and snorkeling. If Unreals isn't cooperating, you can always bodysurf the beachbreak waves up the beach or attempt impossible maneuvers on a bodyboard.

Kealia

Location: Fronting Kuhio Highway north of Kapaa
Activities: Shortboard surfing, longboard surfing, bodyboarding, bodysurfing
Wave: Right and left beachbreak peaks, sometimes hollow
Difficulty: Beginning to expert surfers
Prime time: Breaks all year
Wave range: All swells with any east, 2-6 feet
Amenities: Beachfront parking, nice beach, easy access

Surfers speeding along Kuhio Highway to investigate a rumored north or south swell always ease their foot off the pedal and crane their necks to gape at the ocean when they pass the stretch of beach just north of Kapaa. They usually see some sort of east swell wrapping into the bay being tormented by onshore trade winds, but what they are hoping for is a glimpse of one of those treasured days when a swell is being caressed into loveliness by kona winds.

Early morning or late afternoon windless conditions will also clothe Kealia's beachbreak peaks in a sexy costume of silken glass to help them sing their siren's song of seduction, causing surfers to brake wildly, turn off the highway and scamper into the waves.

Even when wind conditions aren't perfect, Kealia's waves can produce a fun session. On a choppy day when I was killing time watching the uninviting peaks, I noticed that local surfers were catching some wretched-looking waves that miraculously turned into full-bore barrels on the inside section.

It was amazing that these guys could look at these hideous peaks and instinctively know which ones would treat them to a deep tube. Of course, when the winds are perfect it's much easier to figure out which waves will pitch and peel, but Kealia can be fun even when the winds don't cooperate.

Because of Kauai's rounded shape, north swells wrap around the coast and provide some long, peeling lefts at Kealia, while southeast swells stretch the rights into long, workable walls. East swells come pounding straight into the bay to let surfers divide up the equally fine right and left peaks.

Although the entire bay can catch fire at any time, depending on the swell and sandbars, the north end somehow seems to take the ocean's energy and transform it into the juiciest peaks. Numerous theories have been advanced and vigorously defended attributing this wave-enhancement on the north side to the rock jetty, the remnants of a steamer ship landing.

If you are tired of surfing vicious reefs far from shore, Kealia will be a welcome relief, though on bigger days you will be startled by how savagely the waves will batter you as you try to stroke back out to the lineup. It isn't much consolation that you aren't far from shore while the waves treat you to a penetrating saltwater massage.

As the swell gets overhead, the currents will vigorously try to drag you from the lineup and out to sea. To defend your position in the waves, find a good series of objects to line up with on shore, and check them frequently.

The waves at Kealia are willing to display their charms to anyone driving by, and many surfers are more than happy to sample the delights of these fun-loving waves. This means that you won't often be forced to surf these waves alone, but with waves peaking up along a half mile of shoreline, you should be able to find enough waves to keep you smiling.

The Kealia locals are friendly, and most have this place so wired that they'll stupefy you with their mastery of these tricky peaks. While you're ready to chew your fins off in frustration after catching all the wrong waves and missing the good ones, the locals will paddle for a seemingly hopeless lump of a wave that they will somehow squeeze for a double-deep tube ride and add a floater for a flourish at the end.

Getting to the lineup is easy. Just pull off Kuhio Highway and find a strategic place to park. Make sure you hide your key well and leave nothing valuable in your car, or as you're watching the beach between sets you might catch of glimpse of your auto heading down the highway without you.

Study the waves and crowd and pick a peak; then look for discolored and choppy water that indicates a rip current. Start stroking in the rip and let it help you reach the lineup.

Even on smaller days, the current is a cunning beast that will grab you before you know you're being stalked. Don't be fooled by the fun-looking waves and nice beach so reassuringly close. The currents here have snatched many a person who only wanted a bit of fun in the waves and dragged him to a horrid death.

Stay alert, and when the current starts to carry you off, don't panic. Let it carry you beyond the breaking waves and calmly tread water while you decide whether to await rescue or bodysurf the waves to the beach once the current has relaxed its grip.

It's usually worth your small investment in time and energy to check Kealia on your way elsewhere, and if your vision is keen enough to penetrate the waves' disguise, you might be able to see that even when these waves look grumpy, they have a heart of gold.

On a perfect day with offshore winds, even the dullest wit will be sharp enough to scramble into the water to embrace these peaks.

CHAPTER 3

This is the master map of Maui. Consult this map for direction and breakdown of blow-up areas to be shown in the following pages.

HAWAIIAN ISLANDS

125

Lahaina Breakwater

Location: Outside Lahaina Harbor
Activities: Shortboard surfing, longboard surfing, bodyboarding
Wave: Fast performance rights and lefts, sometimes hollow
Difficulty: Beginning to expert surfers
Prime time: Breaks all year
Wave range: South, southwest, north swells, 2-10 feet
Amenities: Parking, nearby restaurants and shops, interesting crowd walking the streets

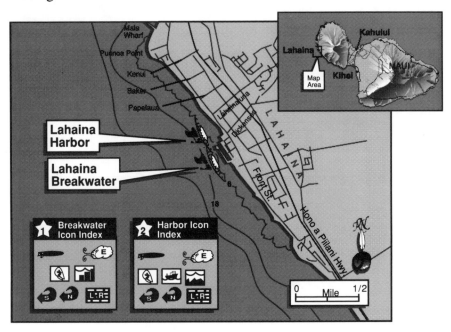

You are certain that a modest little south swell is breaking, and you can hear the faint echoes of a good wave out there somewhere calling you to come play. But everywhere you check, all you see are puny little peaks that are too limp to lure you out into the lineup. Stop wasting time, and haul your okole to the Lahaina Breakwater.

By some mysterious process understood only by serious oceanographers, the reef at the Breakwater will magically produce overhead waves when the rest of the coast strains to come up with ankle snappers.

Whatever the reason, the Lahaina Breakwater is a wave factory that never goes on strike. Summer's south and southwest swells shoot the narrow gap between Kahoolawe and Lanai to produce long, grinding lefts perfect for flashy maneuvers and visits to the tube. Anything is possible on these walls, and the level of surfing in Lahaina is so high you'll probably be inspired to attempt maneuvers that haven't occurred to you in your most crazed daydreams.

During the winter, north swells squeak through the gap between Maui and Molokai and end up as screaming right walls at the Breakwater, a welcome change from summer's lefts.

Molokai and Lanai squat like malevolent bog trolls, preventing west and northwest swells from hitting Lahaina, which is probably fortunate or the Lahaina boys might surf themselves into exhaustion. But the swells that do reach the Breakwater are transformed into perfect platforms from which to launch your most imaginative assaults.

Like most beautiful things, the Breakwater attracts a mob of ardent suitors, keen to partake of that beauty. Competition is fierce to sample the charms of these waves, but after one good ride you'll gladly rejoin the pack for a chance at another taste of pleasure.

The reef fronting the Breakwater is one of those amazing phenomena that can handle 2-foot and 12-foot waves with equal ease, and can cope with almost any swell that makes the hazardous journey through the maze of guardian islands.

Unfortunately, as the swell gets bigger, you'll find it increasingly difficult to resist the efforts of the waves to bash your board and body into the looming rocks of the breakwall.

A snapped leash here has consequences more dire than you'll face at most other surf spots, as even a 2-inch wall of white water is strong enough to speed your board into the rocks. You can collapse a lung swimming frantically after your board only to arrive just in time to watch as the breakwall strips the last inch of fiberglass from your favorite stick.

The trade winds blow offshore here, and make the usually hollow waves even more cavernous. Glassy mornings are a savory morsel reserved for surfers strong-willed enough to shrug off morning lethargy, while sea breezes are punishment for the lazy late-risers.

Any town's popularity is easily measured by how frustrated you become when you try to find parking. By all standards, Lahaina is a wild success. You'll have to be at the waterfront before the mynah birds start squabbling to get a parking spot near the waves, and after 8 a.m. you'll probably have to park blocks away and hike to the Breakwater.

To check the waves and forage for parking, follow Front Street until you reach the Pioneer Inn, and turn down one of the nearby streets. The best way to reach the waves is to walk the breakwater until you are face to face with the waves, and study the surf to find a gap between the peaks. There is no shining silver path to the lineup, so stay alert and look for the channels, and watch the local surfers to see the nooks and crannies they have discovered to escape being caught inside and to return to the lineup easily.

Lahaina Harbor

Location: Right side of Lahaina boat channel
Activities: Shortboard surfing, longboard surfing, bodyboarding
Wave: Fast performance rights and lefts, often hollow
Difficulty: Beginning to expert surfers
Prime time: Breaks all year, summer is best
Wave range: Southwest, south, north swells, 2-8 feet
Amenities: Parking, nearby shops and restaurants

While the Lahaina Harbor channel provides safe passage for a variety of boats, it is also a sanctuary for surfers seeking some summer fun.

South swells give the reef at Lahaina Harbor a wake-up call for prime time action, and southwest swells find that magic lane between Kahoolawe and Lanai to deliver more good waves. You can usually drive to Lahaina on a hunch with little fear of not finding some sort of wave to surf.

The reef here is a voracious creature that will offer you delicious right and left peaks in an effort to lure you close enough to scrape the flesh off your body one painful inch at a time. But by paying careful attention to the tides, you can cheat the reef out of a meal and snatch some choice waves for yourself.

Don't even think of riding the lefts at low tide unless you are growing artificial skin in vats in your private laboratory to replace what the reef flays off you. The low-tide lefts are laced with sharp coral and sea urchins, and your first mistake will leave a bloody mess in the water. Luckily, low tide is the best time for the rights, which will provide hours of painless amusement.

Let your mind go free, and your body will follow. Just make sure no boats drop in on you at Lahaina Harbor. Photo: Erik Aeder

The right at low tide is a steep, wedging peak with an immediate tube followed by a long, playful shoulder as a reward for making it out of the pit. At high tide the right tube vanishes, and the whole wave becomes an ego-pumping performance vehicle. The tube migrates over to the left at high tide, which although still dangerous becomes makable enough to justify the risk.

With a little more water over the reef, these previously horrible pain pits become pleasure peaks. The long, hollow, fast walls will tempt you to push the edge of your ability higher and higher, until you just might amaze yourself with the tracks you lay down. Just don't spoil your fun by trying to walk on the reef after a wipeout, or the coral and sea urchins will send you hobbling to the beach in agony.

Unless you are keen for full-moon surf sessions, you will have to share these beauties with a horde of hungry surfers. This is one of the southwest shore's main surf attractions, and Lahaina has a large population of resident surfers.

Every wave and every swell is picked clean, but with luck, patience and cunning you should be able to get your share. The trade winds blow offshore here, making the already hollow waves even more cavernous and clean. Glassy mornings and evenings are an extra-fine treat, and only afternoon sea breezes and rare kona winds make these waves unridable.

Possibly the best time to score uncrowded waves at Lahaina Harbor is in the fall, winter or spring when a straight north swell runs the blockade of Molokai and slips into Lahaina unmolested.

Getting to the lineup is easy,; just paddle out through the boat channel and take evasive action when motorized watercraft threaten to dice you with their propellers.

The rights end when they hit the deep water of the channel, while the lefts keep going as long as you are game. While getting back out to the rights is a cruise in the channel, returning to the lefts involves careful stroking over sharp coral.

Honolua Bay

Location: North of Kapalua Golf Course
Activities: Shortboard surfing, bodyboarding
Wave: Ultimate long performance right, often hollow
Difficulty: Intermediate to expert surfers
Prime time: September through April
Wave range: Straight west, big northwest, or north swells, 3-20 feet
Amenities: Cliff-top parking, excellent view

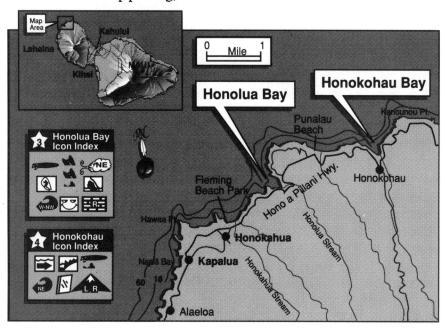

Once you've tasted a wave at Honolua Bay you will endure any hardship for another taste. Lie, cheat, steal, whatever it takes, you'll gladly pay the price to plug into Honolua's power lines.

Honolua has ample doses of what all surfers crave: power, speed, and tube time, all wrapped up in an attractive package of long, peeling walls. Honolua is one of the top competitors for the title of best wave in the Islands, and it presses that claim by satisfying a wide variety of surfers.

The view of Honolua Bay from the pineapple fields atop the cliff is one of the most inspirational sights in surfing. Lines come sweeping in from the open ocean and start peeling as they hit Coconuts on the far point. The waves continue to peel as they wrap into the cove at Outside, and by the time they reach the Cave they are snarling, spitting beasts as they wind their way into the deeper water of the bay and churn themselves into a quiet death.

But before they die, any surfer skillful enough to latch onto a wave will be forced to pull out every item from his bag of tricks. On the cliffs above,

130

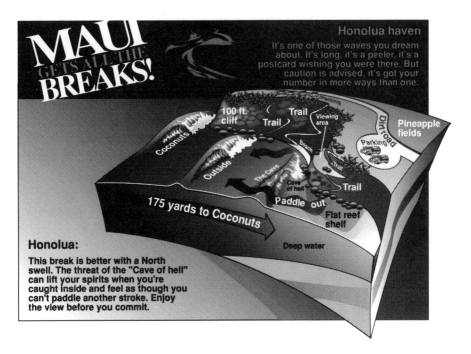

Honolua haven

It's one of those waves you dream about. It's long, it's a peeler, it's a postcard wishing you were there. But caution is advised, it's got your number in more ways than one.

100 ft. cliff

Trail

Trail

Viewing area

Dirt road

Pineapple fields

Coconuts

Outside

Beach

Parking

The Cave

Cave of hell

Trail

Trail

175 yards to Coconuts

Paddle out

Flat reef shelf

Honolua:

This break is better with a North swell. The threat of the "Cave of hell" can lift your spirits when you're caught inside and feel as though you can't paddle another stroke. Enjoy the view before you commit.

Deep water

the gallery will be scrutinizing every move, hoping to be amazed. Surfers paddling out have the perfect perspective to analyze the whole ride. If you blow it, you can be certain that your disgrace will be remembered the next time you paddle for a wave.

When the surf is 3 to 5 feet, you will be convinced you have stumbled onto hot-doggers' heaven. The waves provide enough juice and speed to carry you through any maneuver imaginable, interrupted only by visits to the tube. If you just feel like cruising on these long walls, that's OK too, as Honolua has a way of making the most mundane maneuvers magical.

At 6 to 10 feet the waves begin to impose their will, and the rides become less flashy and more functional. Down-the-line moves are essential to beat the sections and make the tubes.

When the waves get this big everyone starts thinking about the cave. This board-devouring hole in the cliff is surely the lair of the hellhounds that guard the Gates of Hades. The cave is the waking nightmare of every surfer whose leash has snapped or who has been dragged by the white water to pay a painful visit to this troll's den.

You board will probably plead for rescue if a wave snaps your leash and drags the board for a tour of the cave, but don't listen. You can always get another board, while your body will take a long, painful time to heal.

Numerous boards have been devoured and bodies battered in the cave, but escape is possible. When you wipe out or get caught inside, aim your

131

board past the cave's gaping mouth and let the white water take you toward the bay. If the surge is taking you straight for the cave, abandon your board and spread your arms and legs as a sea anchor. When the wave passes, stroke wildly past the cave's mouth toward the bay.

A few times a year 12- to 20-foot swells pay a visit to Honolua Bay and put on a show that from the cliff looks spectacular, while from the water will make every atom in your body tingle with fear and the thrill of being alive.

Straight west swells shoot the gap between Lanai and Molokai, while huge northwest swells bull their way past Molokai's east end and wrap into Honolua Bay. North swells also slip past Molokai and funnel into the Bay. When Oahu's North Shore is blasted by a giant northwest swell, many surfers zip over to Maui where the Bay will turn the swells into long, fast walls.

The valley walls herd the trade winds offshore at Honolua, which ensures that most swells are blessed with good winds and clean waves.

Once you pull off Honoapiilani Highway onto the dirt road through the pineapple fields and find a place to park, you'll notice that you are high above the waves. Several paths lead down to the surf, and the quickest way down is to slip at the top of the trail and fall to the bottom. However, you'll be in no shape to surf, so make your way down carefully and slowly.

The easiest way out to the lineup is to take the trail closest to the inner bay and launch into the water from the rocks. This puts you on top of the shallow inside section, but by this point the waves have been drained of most of their destructive energy and you can stroke across the shelf to deeper water and then watch the action as you make the long paddle to the lineup.

Some surfers prefer the thrill of taking one of the paths to the cove between Outside and the Cave and trying to time the sets to paddle out during a lull. Bad timing or bad luck means a quick visit to the cave.

One wave at the Bay and you'll forget your own name in your haste to paddle back out and grab another. Photo: Erik Aeder.

The most difficult thing about Honolua is deciding which peak to ride. No matter how much fun you're having in the waves, the peak farther over will always appear to be just a little bit bigger, faster or hollower. Coconuts is less protected by the cliffs, so it is usually choppier. But the waves are biggest out here as they begin their long wrap into the Bay.

The peak at Outside is cleaner, though slightly smaller and less powerful than Coconuts, but if you don't make the wave you'll be heading for the cave.

The Cave is cleanest and hollowest, though the wave has lost some size by the time it wraps this far. This is also where the crowd is thickest. Under 8 feet, each of these spots is a distinct peak, but as the waves get bigger the peaks join together into one long, mind-blowing speed run. If you're fast enough.

Unfortunately, everyone who has had a good day at the Bay is turned into a zombie with one controlling thought: "I must get more waves at the Bay." Some people devote their entire surfing experience to riding Honolua Bay, and with so many admirers, the Bay is usually crowded.

It's possible to score waves at Honolua, but Lady Luck has to be intensely interested in your life. You can give her a hand by surfing the Bay early in the morning, or anticipating a swell and hitting the water before the ravening hordes are alerted.

Honokohau

Location: Next bay north of Honolua, along Honoapiilani Highway
Activities: Shortboard surfing, longboard surfing, bodyboarding
Wave: Fun river mouth rights and lefts
Difficulty: Beginning to intermediate surfers
Prime time: September through April
Wave range: All swells with any north, 2-8 feet
Amenities: Beachfront parking, solitude, great scenery

Sometimes modern life becomes so hectic that you just can't stand to look at another neon wetsuit or see hordes of surfers hassling each other for waves and you want to flee to some secluded spot to kick back and do some serious nonserious surfing.

Honokohau Bay is just such a refuge where you can regain your sanity and enjoy a little peace of mind in a serene setting. You will never hear the name Honokohau spoken around the campfire when surfers swap lies about the great waves they've ridden. But this means you won't see swarms of wave snatchers polluting the lineup at Honokohau either.

The beach is of the coarse-grained variety, composed mainly of fist-sized rocks that become actual boulders in the wave zone. This bottom can be deftly arranged by the stream and winter waves into a shoal that can force the waves to form fun rights and lefts, perfect for longboard cruising or shortboard shredding, as the mood suits you. Bodyboarders will also find Honokohau an accommodating host for their frantic antics.

Although the water is generally murky, sharks are not a problem here, and the only real hazard is the vigorous current that is created when the waves get big. The ridable walls usually go into hiding when the swell gets serious, and surfers who are lured into the lineup when the waves are big risk being kidnapped by the current and taken on a harrowing tour of the inhospitable cliffs that guard the coast on each side of Honokohau Bay.

Although the trade winds usually blow sideshore here, the cliffs provide some protection from the disruptive effect of the wind and make the waves fun if not fantastic. When the winds abate or blow kona, the waves can do a reasonable impersonation of your basic superior beach break.

The waves at Honokohau change as often as a Tasmanian she-devil, so you never know what to expect when you drive up the short beach road from Honoapiilani Highway. When the waves are grumpy and frumpy, you can still manage to have a good time fooling around on fun waves in an unspoiled tropical setting. And when everything comes together for a magical session, you'll find it easy to weave a spell with your board. Rights, lefts, left-go-rights, tubes, long walls--it's easy to have a good time when no one is battling you for waves.

Hookipa

Location: Off Hookipa Beach Park just past Paia on Hana Highway

Activities: Shortboard surfing, longboard surfing, bodyboarding, sailboarding

Wave: Fast performance right and left peaks, often hollow

Difficulty: Intermediate to expert surfers

Prime time: Breaks all year

Wave range: Northwest, north, northeast, east, east-southeast swells, 2-18 feet

Amenities: Beachfront parking, restrooms, showers, excellent view from parking lots

Offshore of Hookipa Beach Park on Maui's northeast shore fierce battles are waged while most tourists exclaim "Look at all those people in the water having fun." The battleground is a series of surf spots and the warriors are surfers and sailboarders jousting for Maui's most consistent waves.

Luckily, the same wind conditions that make the waves prime for surfing render them useless for sailboarders, and the sailboarders are happiest when the palm trees are bent to the ground by howling trade winds while surfers sit beached by the whitecaps.

Many a battle is fought when wind conditions are somewhere between those extremes, with the surfers being outgunned by the quicker and more maneuverable sailboarders. The wave sailors can get you coming and going as they jump the waves heading out to sea and zip along on the ride to shore. If you've ever been surfing when a flock of sailboarders swoops, you know how confusing and maddening it is to have them soaring down from the skies while you are busy scanning the horizon for a set.

Hookipa is a wave machine that produces good, overhead surf all year long in exhausting quantities. The sailboarders dominate when the trade winds are blowing, and sit sullenly on the beach during kona or glassy days while the surfers are shredding the peaks. On days of light trade winds, both groups either share the peaks, or stick with their own kind at each peak.

Most sailboarders shun Pavilions at the east side of the bay, as the winds are erratic and the waves infested by surfers. The cliffs beside Pavilions shelter the waves from the trades and provide clean conditions while nearby spots are in tatters from those same winds.

Pavilions is the most heavily surfed spot at Hookipa because it is such an easy wave and maintains a high fun quotient. These fun rights break up against the cliff and zip along to a safe channel that also provides a safe, quick return to the lineup.

Although low tide can force the waves to pitch and tube, Pavilions is mostly a high-performance wall that will pump up your ego. You can bend these accommodating waves to your will without any fear that they might rebel and cause you pain. You would have to be pretty pathetic as well as incredibly unlucky to get hurt here, as the waves take you away from the rocks along the point. Just to make sure no one gets hurt here, Pavilions closes out over 6 feet, sending surfers across the channel to Middles for a thrill.

On a north swell Middles gives surfers a choice, either a short but intense right or a long but intense left that can handle swells up to 12 feet. Sailboarders usually prefer the rights, and the wind frequently blows wrong for them to take advantage of the superior lefts. This gives surfers a good chance to surf unmolested, and they make good use of this advantage by shredding the long lefts. However, since Middles breaks so far out into the bay the usual trades can turn a serious swell into a swirling mass of white water. Early mornings and late afternoons are the best time to ambush ridable waves at Middles.

Off the west end of the bay lurks the Point, a great right/left combination that gives most surfers an overdose of excitement. The wave splits into a right that breaks off a rocky point and into a channel that provides easy access back to the lineup, while the lefts peel into a channel in the bay. The right is vastly superior to the left, but the price of failure is higher than most surfers are willing to pay.

The relentless surge of the current and the white water drags horrified surfers and sailboarders into a ravenous pile of rocks that thrives on surfboards and sailboard rigs. The shallowest section of reef lurks directly in front of the rocks just to make sure they are well fed, so that your ride is often interrupted by the wave pitching out over this wicked reef.

Although the rocks gobble up surfboards and sailboarders with equal relish, they have a preference for the more expensive rigs of the sailboarders, who can lose thousands of dollars worth of equipment on a bad day.

The other problem with the Point is that it is infested with sailboarders, as the trades blow perfectly for their purposes and they regard it as one of the finest sailboard spots in the world. Although the long, fast, hollow right is worth enduring a lot of grief for the rush it provides, when the sailboarders are out in force it's better to retreat to the cliff-top parking lot to watch the greatest sailboarding show on Earth.

Study this photo well, for it's a sight you'll seldom see: a wave at Hookipa unmolested by surfers or sailboarders. Photo: Erik Aeder

When the ocean is in a surly mood and bashes Pavilions into oblivion with a brute of a swell, it makes up for it by resurrecting the slumbering reef at the Lane, just west across the channel from the Point. The Lane is one of those spots where you spend long, thoughtful moments checking your equipment and attitude before you hit the water.

The powerful currents aroused by a big swell churn through the lineup and out to sea, and the rocky point looms ominously to welcome you if you wipe out or are caught inside. Fear can cause you to hear the rocks gnashing their teeth in anticipation as the white water drags you toward their foam-flecked jaws.

This long, hideous beast of a left will let you know immediately if you don't have the right equipment or your surfing ability is deficient in any way. The trouble is, by the time the waves punish you for your impertinence, it may be too late.

There are no lifeguards here, and most surfers and sailboarders are having enough trouble coping with these rugged waves to risk injury by saving your pitiful okole. The most important decision you can make here is whether to paddle out at the Lane, and if any doubts are whispering in the back of your brain, listen to them a little longer while you see how everyone else is coping with the waves.

If you can handle the Lane and its power, it's a rush that will have all your nerve circuits firing with maximum efficiency.

Getting to Hookipa is easier than getting out to the waves. Just cruise Hana Highway out of Kahului until you pass the colorful town of Paia. Continue along the Hana Highway a few more miles until you see a beautiful bay spread out between two points and parking lots jammed with cars. This is Hookipa Beach Park, the epicenter of surfing and sailboarding on Maui.

The most strategic parking spot depends on which peak you want to surf. The east parking lot gives a great view of Pavilions and the rest of the bay looking west, while the point parking lot puts you right atop the action at the Lane and the Point. The lower lots at sea level near the beach put you closer to the showers and launching areas.

The narrow, sandy beach has a flat section of rocky shelf just offshore, which makes paddling out somewhat tricky. If you intend to surf Pavilions, the best place to launch is from the beach just ashore on the east end of the bay. Just let the current help you reach the lineup.

The safest way to reach the Point and the Lane is to paddle out from the west end of the bay and use the currents and channels to assist you to the lineup. If you want to emulate the Maui boys, just keep in mind that these guys are rugged characters who have been surfing these waves for years, and know every trick to keep from getting pounded while paddling out. They usually reach the Lane and the Point by paddling out from a rocky cove just around the point, but while this route is shorter, the penalty for failure is a terrifying backward trip to the rocks.

Although it's a rare day any time of year that one of Hookipa's spots isn't going off, the winds determine whether the surfers or sailboarders will rule. The trades blow most vigorously during the summer, while the fall, winter and spring months are blessed with many kona wind days, or special days when the winds are calm and the waves perfect.

Honomanu

Location: Between Kaumahina State Park and Keanae
Activities: Shortboard surfing, long-board surfing, bodyboarding
Wave: River mouth lefts, cliffside rights, sometimes hollow
Difficulty: Beginning to expert surfers
Prime time: Breaks all year
Wave range: North, northeast, east, east-southeast swells, 3-10 feet
Amenities: Parking, exotic setting, freshwater river

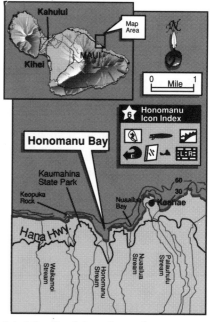

The northeast coast of Maui is hostile to surfers, jealously guarding its treasures with rugged cliffs and steep valleys. The few accessible waves here are shredded by constant onshore trade winds, and the twisting roads force you to travel 20 miles to reach bays only five miles apart.

Nestled beneath the steep cliffs is Honomanu, a jewel of a bay. While the trade winds lacerate other nearby surf spots, Honomanu's waves are sheltered by the valley walls. Although it takes a fair bit of a drive along the tortuous Hana Highway to reach Honomanu, the reward is apparent once you pull up to the beach.

To the left of the river mouth is a left peak that is usually a performance wave, but can get hollow when the river arranges the rocky shoal correctly. Even when the waves aren't hollow, the left is good for exciting walls and juicy sections. The river water makes wiping out here a refreshing change from the usual saltwater bath.

Farther out on the right side of the bay is a rocky reef that provides some wonderful peaks and rippable walls that can get hollow at low tide.

The wave peaks up beside a steep cliff, which makes for a curious sensation as you watch the water rising up the cliff face while you stroke for a wave that lifts you up the cliff as well. The drop is a quick plunge down a steep wave face, followed by a fast tube and long wall. The presence of a rock-lined cove in front of you will lend your trip to the tube a sense of urgency well beyond the usual desire to emerge from the barrel in style. The threat of being caught inside and dragged toward the rocks will inspire you to paddle with admirable efficiency.

Other than the rock gauntlet, Honomanu is very forgiving when you wipe out, although when the wave is holding you down you might be startled by the sound of the waves cracking rocks together underwater. Overhead waves generate a fierce seaward current, but the bay is deep and wide enough to let you escape the rip by paddling to either side of the bay.

Just before Keanae as the Hana Highway finally turns back to the coast, at the bottom of a hairpin turn take the short dirt road to the river mouth. You will immediately know whether you are going to surf that day.

Although not a world-class wave, Honomanu is usually fun, and with an overhead swell and calm wind, the waves will make you glad you're alive and surfing. This is Hawaiian surfing at its best: no crowds, and good waves in a tree-lined tropical bay.

And if you easily master the rights and lefts inside the bay and begin to crave more excitement, a greater challenge awaits. On the outside edge of the bay beneath formidable cliffs a left beckons, a wave that comes alive when a giant swell coincides with kona or calm winds. Few surfers accept the challenge.

Right this moment there is a wave peeling on Maui just for you. To find it, keep your eyes open and trust your instincts. Photo: Erik Aeder

140

CHAPTER 4

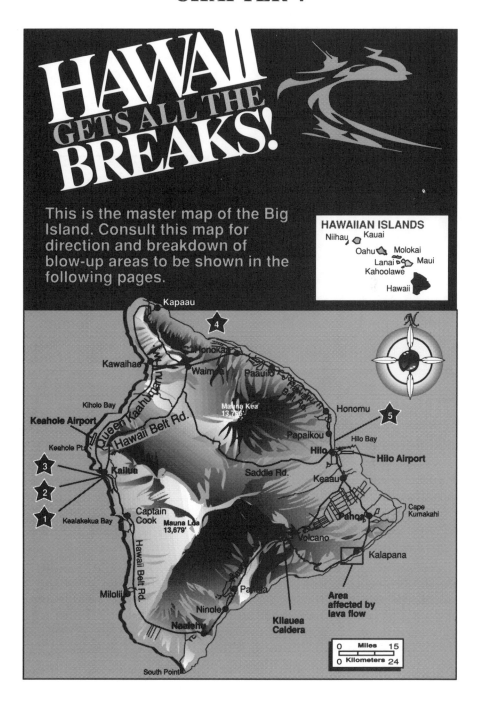

HAWAII GETS ALL THE BREAKS!

This is the master map of the Big Island. Consult this map for direction and breakdown of blow-up areas to be shown in the following pages.

HAWAIIAN ISLANDS

Niihau · Kauai
Oahu · Molokai
Lanai · Maui
Kahoolawe
Hawaii

Kapaau

Kawaihae

Kiholo Bay

Keahole Airport

Keahole Pt.

Kailua

Kealakekua Bay

Captain Cook

Mauna Loa
13,679'

Milolii

Ninole

Naalehu

South Point

Honokaa

Waimea

Paauilo

Mauna Kea
13,796'

Honomu

Papaikou

Hilo Bay

Hilo

Hilo Airport

Saddle Rd.

Keaau

Pahoa

Volcano

Cape Kumakahi

Kalapana

Area affected by lava flow

Pahala

Kilauea Caldera

Queen Kaahumanu

Hawaii Belt Rd.

Hawaii Belt Rd.

| 0 | Miles | 15 |
| 0 | Kilometers | 24 |

Lymans

Location: South of Banyans, north side of Kamoa Point in Kailua-Kona
Activities: Shortboard surfing, longboard surfing, bodyboarding
Wave: Long left wall, sometimes hollow
Difficulty: Beginning to expert surfers
Prime time: Breaks all year
Wave range: South, southwest, west, northwest swells, 4-12 feet
Amenities: Beachfront parking, supreme viewing from shore

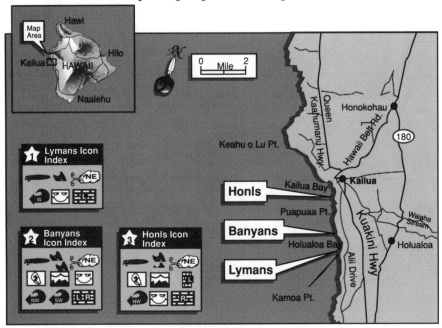

Depending on what time of year you surf the lefts that break off the south side of Holualoa Bay, you will either disdain the spot as a haven for wimps or praise it as a thrilling pleasure-drome.

As you drive along Kailua's scenic Alii Drive, Holualoa Bay will grab your eyes and force them to admire the area's beauty as you idly muse that waves would do wonders to make the spot more picturesque.

Summertime brings south and southwest swells that improve the scenery considerably, until you take your board into the lineup and realize that these gutless walls are more suitable for beginners and other surfers who don't need much of a thrill factor to make them happy in the waves.

Winter's west and northwest swells boost the thrill factor at Lymans dramatically and change summer's slow, insipid peaks into fierce waves with a steep drop, fast wall and hollow sections. During the winter, a good leash will keep your board from feeding the voracious rocks that line the bay.

The shallow reef off the point is always hungry for human flesh, especially when the hulking waves of winter body slam you onto the coral, but the deep water of the bay provides a good refuge after a wipeout or closeout set and an easy route back to the lineup.

Beginners will have a great time cruising on the lefts at Lymans during summer funtime, and the slow walls are perfect places to develop the skills that will save your life when winter's head-cracking waves start coming ashore. The trade winds blow most often during the summer, but as they are offshore on the Kona side, this just makes the waves hold up longer and helps create the occasional tube.

Wintertime is plagued with more-frequent kona storms, with the accompanying irksome onshore winds and driving rain, but winter makes amends by producing more clean, calm mornings where the waves become walls of liquid glass.

On a glassy morning with an overhead west or northwest swell, Lymans will treat you to a neck-wrenching steep takeoff, followed by a quick tube and long, fast wall that tapers finely as the wave wraps into the deeper water of the bay.

Parking is available right along Alii Drive at Lymans, which is named after the nearby Lyman family home. The whole bayfront becomes an auditorium as people line Alii Drive and the undeveloped state land at Kamoa Point to watch the big waves come booming into the bay.

Getting to the lineup is simple; just pick your way through the rocks to the water and stroke casually out through the deep water of the bay, safe from the watery claws of the waves. The paddle back out after a wave is enlivened by the view of other surfers, who just might inspire you to new heights of performance with their ride.

Banyans

Location: Fronting Kona Bali Kai condo on Alii Drive
Activities: Shortboard surfing, longboard surfing, bodyboarding
Wave: Fast performance lefts and rights, often hollow
Difficulty: Beginning to expert surfers
Prime time: Breaks all year
Wave range: South, southwest, west, northwest swells, 2-10 feet
Amenities: Beachfront parking, nearby market

If you need more proof that God possesses a biting sense of humor, consider that the Big Island's finest surf spot is located in the area with the fastest-growing population. As an added touch of irony, Banyans is easily visible from Alii Drive, and a market is located across the street so surfers can get lubricated before and after each session.

Named after the impressive tree that marks the entrance to the waves, Banyans is forced by its favorable location to endure the presence of surfers all year.

Summer's south and southwest swells bring the lefts to life with long walls and hollow sections that stop peeling when they enter the deeper water of a little bay. The rights are ridable during summer swells, but aren't as long or as desirable as the lefts, which makes them a good option for surfers who occupy the spot near the bottom of the pecking order.

When winter starts delivering west and northwest swells, the rights become the supreme attraction, with long, fast walls and tubes galore. The reef here will make you painfully aware of the tide, and as there is no channel on the rights you will do well to consider each maneuver in terms of how likely you are to make it, and how badly you don't want to leave skin on the coral.

At high tide the waves will permit you to attempt any hair-brained maneuver that might suggest itself to you without making you pay too severe a price. Because they end in such a good channel, the lefts are always forgiving.

At low tide the rights will bait a trap with insanely hollow sections to lure you into the pit, and when the trap snaps shut the waves bash you off your board and drag you off helplessly to be skinned by the reef. After one low-tide wipeout you'll probably start to flinch whenever the wave tempts you with a tube, or opt to sip a cool drink on the beach as you wait for high tide to provide a cushion of comfort over the reef.

Although rocky and devoid of sand, the shore provides a splendid viewing area to watch surfers making a blood sacrifice for some low-tide tubes.

The wind patterns in Kona are among the best in the state for surfing. Mornings usually dawn bright and clear with waves smooth and desirable in the early morning glass. When the winds pick up later in the day, they are usually offshore and make the waves hollower.

As is depressingly predictable with a good surf spot in a populated area, nary a wave makes it to shore without being slashed by surfers. The feeding pattern here resembles the dining etiquette observed by a pride of lions after a large kill on the African savanna.

The shy, timid surfers arrive at dawn and grab whatever they can before the bad boys show up and chase them away. After a while the very bad boys arrive and wrest the waves away from the bad boys, who retire to the beach grumbling. Much later, after the very bad boys have terrorized the waves awhile, the extremely very bad boys finally show up to seize control of the lineup and ravage the waves.

When this ultimate group of predators arrives you might as well paddle in and wait your chance to slink back into the lineup after they have departed, as you won't even be able to snatch a few leftover scraps. With constant vigilance and terrible patience your time will come, and the wait will certainly be worth it.

When a brute of a swell over 10 feet starts rampaging down the coast, the reef goes into a protective coma and the waves close out all the way south to Lymans in nearby Holualoa Bay.

This doesn't happen too often, however, because the northwest swells release most of their fury pounding the other islands, and by the time they make their way south to the Big Island and wrap down the coast to Kona, they are too exhausted to do more than deliver a token head slap to the reef at Banyans.

After securing your car along Alii Drive, the best route to the waves is to paddle out through the channel in the little cove that marks the end of the lefts. Although the channel is well-defined, it is mined with coral heads, so be alert, especially at low tide.

The rights have no channel, and returning to the lineup after a wave is easy if you hit the water in mid-stroke after a flyaway kickout. Getting back out after a wipeout is a bit more strenuous.

If you aren't too badly maimed by the reef and keen to give the coral another shot at your body, time the sets well and stroke like mad during a lull. If it's too shallow to duck-dive through a wave, just brace yourself and hang on to your board as the wave detonates on your head.

If the swell isn't too big or the tide isn't too low, the waves will merely make you earn the right to surf them. Otherwise, they will punish you for being bold enough to challenge them, and only the fittest surfers end up with the lion's share of the waves.

Honls

Location: South of Hilton Hotel along Alii drive, Kailua-Kona
Activities: Shortboard surfing, longboard surfing, bodyboarding
Wave: Fast performance rights and lefts, often hollow
Difficulty: Beginning to expert surfers
Prime time: Breaks all year
Wave range: South, southwest, west, northwest swells, 3-7 feet, southwest is best
Amenities: Beachfront parking

Although almost everyone has Honls easily classified as a fun small-wave playground, the spot suffers an identity crisis.

Surfers call it everything from Haddos to Hannos, but it is actually named after the nearby Honl family home. Whatever you call it, the spot is a year-round source of surfing pleasure.

When the waves are shoulder high and smaller, the bodyboarders infest the waves and drive the surfers crazy with amazing antics that would leave the surfer that attempted the same tricks contorted and perforated.

When the wave hits the reef it jacks up in a right/left peak that lets cooperative surfers divvy up the loot and each enjoy a good ride. On those maddening occasions when some twit cuts you off it's good to have the option to go the other way and get a good ride.

Some riders swear by the rights, while others will defend the lefts with their dying breath, but each swell brings out the best in each direction, depending on the swell direction.

Although the waves break comfortingly close to shore, the beach is a rock-lined wall of misery and the reef is a board- and body-lacerating creature that can be your worst nightmare at low tide. High tide brings out the crowds, so if you don't mind sacrificing yourself and your board you can usually get some waves to yourself at low tide.

As the swell gets bigger the board surfers become more serious and chase the bodyboarders away so they can enjoy the fast, hollow walls unmolested.

Hardly a swell is wasted in Kailua-Kona, as the trade winds blow offshore, and this coast is blessed with numerous glassy mornings and evenings. Winter kona storms turn the waves into unridable junk, but the reef can accommodate such a wide variety of swells that you are usually going to score good surf when you check Honls.

As you pass the Hilton heading south on Alii Drive, look for a bunch of seemingly derelict cars parked by a low wall next to a break in the beach foliage. This is the access and paddle out zone, as well as a good place to watch after you've caught your share of waves and your limp arms won't let you paddle back out for just one more.

Waipio

Location: Waipio river mouth, end of the road north of Honokaa
Activities: Shortboard surfing, longboard surfing, bodyboarding, bodysurfing
Wave: Right and left beachbreak peaks, sometimes hollow
Difficulty: Beginning to expert surfers
Prime time: Breaks all year
Wave range: North, northeast, east swells, 2-7 feet
Amenities: Isolated beach, no crowds, freshwater stream

I met Eric Roberts when he was a University of Hawaii student living on Oahu, and was intrigued by his surfing style. Timing, wave judgment, power and grace--he had them all in abundance.

I couldn't imagine where he had developed such a pleasing technique, and was astounded when he told me that he grew up in Kamuela on the Big Island and perfected his style at Wapio Bay. I would have been less amazed if he had told me he was raised by a talking pack of wild dogs that taught him the secrets of the ocean during moonlight bodysurfing sessions.

Wapio Valley is an hour's drive from Kamuela, and the steep road is accessible only by foot, mule, or 4-wheel drive. How did this kid ever beg, borrow or steal rides to Waipio often enough to become so good? While the river mouth is good for a fun session in the beachbreak peaks most of the year, it is somewhat deficient as a training ground for champion surfers.

Waipio Valley is much more than a surf destination; it's a trip into Hawaii's past that provides an intimate glimpse into the heart of Hawaii. If you plan a few day's camping and hiking adventure to supplement your surf sessions here, you just might be touched by the same feelings of aloha for this lovely valley that have inspired so many songwriters, poets and writers.

A black sand beach is but a remnant of the vast sand dunes that the ocean has stripped from the beach and deposited offshore to provide a generous supply of sand that currents turn into migrating sandbars. These shifting sand shoals create an ever-changing cast of waves all year and make each day's surf session wonderfully different.

In the summertime, constant trade winds and the occasional hurricane provide fun waves custom-designed for frantic beachbreak slashing sessions. Winter brings bigger swells that usually overpower the sandbars and create a fearsome shore pound that dares you to try and ride it. Anyone foolish enough to accept that dare would be instantly swept away along a treacherous, cliff-lined coast by vicious currents, never to be seen again.

But on a rising or dying winter swell, the beachbreak can present some inspirational peaks and sections, especially early in the morning or late in the afternoon when the winds are calm.

When a swell 6 feet or smaller shows up at the same time as kona winds, the resulting waves will beckon to you with open barrels and long, smooth right and left walls. This is a special treat on the Big Island, as beaches and especially beachbreaks are as rare as an original thought.

Although the discharge from the Waipio Stream makes the water murky, sharks are not a problem. However, there are usually so few people in the water that it will be impossible to keep your thoughts from straying to vivid images of the last *National Geographic* special you saw featuring Great Whites devouring bloody seal carcasses.

Waipio Valley is guarded by a steep, narrow road that only 4-wheel-drive vehicles are allowed to tackle. To reach the Waipio lookout, follow Highway 19 (Hawaii Belt Road) until it intersects Highway 240, then cruise through Honokaa to the lookout.

If you lack a suitable vehicle for the trip into the valley but are keen to surf the waves, you can usually charm someone into giving you a ride down in their rig. Failing that, you can walk, which has the advantage of allowing you to enjoy the view at a leisurely pace.

The ultimate way to savor the surf at Waipio is to plan to camp in the valley for a few days, to experience what life in Hawaii must have been like before modern life made everything so hectic.

And as you paddle in from a fun session in the beachbreak, the thought may haunt you too: how did Eric Roberts get so good?

Honolii

Location: A few miles north of Hilo
Activities: Shortboard surfing, longboard surfing, bodyboarding
Wave: Fast performance left, often hollow, short fun rights
Difficulty: Beginning to expert surfers
Prime time: Breaks all year
Wave range: North, northeast, east, east-southeast swells, 2-12 feet, northeast is best
Amenities: Parking, showers, restrooms, paved path to beach, interesting beach, great scenery

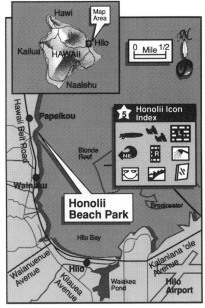

The cool waters of the Honolii Stream faithfully carry a precious cargo of sediment and rocks to Honolii Bay. It's almost a game, with the raging winter swells stripping the beach and the stream replenishing the sediment.

No one would ever pay attention to this ages-old contest if it weren't for the waves. Without the stream's cargo of movable material, the beach and shoals would disappear, and the waves would have won the final game. Except that the ridable waves would also disappear, and Hilo's surfers would lose their most productive wave playground.

When a development company tried to create a hydroelectric power plant upstream with a catchment basin that would have halted the downstream flow of sediment and rocks, the area's surfers and environmentalists quickly perceived the peril. They clamored so loudly and effectively that the state stepped in and nixed the power plant. Because of that vigilance, you will have a chance to surf one of the Big Island's favored waves.

During the summer the trade winds blow up constant swells, supplemented by the rare hurricane and east-southeast groundswells from Southern Hemisphere storms. When kona winds or smooth conditions greet these swells the resulting waves are sexy enough to star in your midnight dreams.

When winter arrives, surfing at Honolii becomes hectic as strong north, northeast and east swells bull their way into the bay and make every session an adventure in survival. Winter usually has a gratifying number of glassy mornings and evenings that will hide the waves' bestial nature under a mask of silky smooth water.

As the main surf playground of the populous Hilo area, Honolii is usually crowded. But even at its worst, a Big Island crowd is much more mellow and friendly than any crowd on Oahu.

Honolii Stream creates a horrendous bowl on the north side of the bay where it deposits its load of sediment into a shoal. After you make a steep drop on the left peak outside the point and jam across the long wall, the sight of the looming bowl will inspire you to turn on the afterburners. Your choices when you reach the bowl are slam or be slammed, and your response will tell you heaps about your surfing philosophy. Some incredible specimens of surfers grin maniacally as they launch into a floater or tuck into a seemingly impossible tube, while others make a feeble attempt at some ill-advised maneuver and brace for the beating.

At 6 feet and under these waves are playful little creatures that are eager to show you a good time, despite the menace of the closeout in the shorebreak and the rock-lined shore. The wave starts outside the north end of the bay with a steep drop and long, peeling wall that tapers as it heads to the shorebreak and offers plenty of opportunity to bail out.

If you're alert you can snag a few good rights, but don't forget to pull out before you reach the rocks on the point.

As the waves get bigger, the crowd becomes smaller as the waves beat the enthusiasm out of them. The right wave will line up all down the beach, while the wrong wave will permit only a few quick turns before it closes out.

On double overhead days all the lefts end in a dumping closeout that will separate you from your board, and the halves of your board from each other. This hideous closeout section snaps dozens of boards on a big day, but that's only if you can make it to the lineup. The shorebreak becomes a nasty barrier when the waves are big, and will bash you each time you try to return to the lineup after a wave.

The current is a predictable creature that runs seaward and over to the north point. If it snatches you, don't panic and struggle against it. Either let it carry you outside the bay and patiently await rescue, or let it carry you to the waves and bodysurf them to the beach. If the worst happens, at least your body won't disappear. The current deposits the ocean's victims in almost the same spot, and searchers know just where to look.

To reach Honolii Beach Park, turn off the Belt Highway at Nahala Street, or turn inland at Paukaa and follow the old road to the coast.

If even the biggest, nastiest day at Honolii is too easy, another challenge that might interest you is Tombstones, around the point toward Hilo. The takeoff zone is a short paddle around the point from Honolii, and this grinding left point wave breaks beneath imposing vertical cliffs.

If you have to straighten out there, the waves will merely be amused by your pathetic attempts to avoid being dashed against the cliffs and will speed you to your doom more quickly. A dominating session at Tombstones earns you immediate entry into the bad boys club.

HAWAII GETS ALL THE BREAKS!

Honolii dream
Ever get a chance to surf inside a postcard? Here's your chance. But make sure you remember, postage isn't paid.

Honolii Point

Tombstones 200 yards

50 ft. cliff

50 ft. cliff

Paddle out

Short rights

Paddle out

Bowl

About 30 yards

Honolii Stream

Pebble beach

Honolii:
This break gets better with a medium swell. Currents are tricky. You can catch a ride on the stream's current on the way out.

150

SURF SHOPS

Honolulu

Blue Planet
813 Kapahulu Ave., 922-5444
Rentals, lessons, new/used longboards, shortboards, board repairs.

Classic Surfboards
842-4761
Makes surfboards; repair service

Downing Hawaii, Get Wet
3021 Waialae Ave., 737-9696
Sells & rents surfboards, bodyboards; surf accessories, clothing; repair service (Downing boards only)

Fresh Wave
1269 S. Beretania St., 593-2936
Sells custom, stock surfboards, bodyboards, surf accessories, canoe accessories, clothing

Hawaiian Island Creations
Ala Moana Shopping Cntr., 941-4491
Sells surfboards, bodyboards, surf accessories, clothing; repair service

Russ-K Quiksilver Boardriders Club
1714 Kapiolani Blvd., 951-7877
Sells custom longboards, bodyboards, used surfboards, clothing, surf accessories

Town & Country Surf Shop
Ala Moana Shopping Cntr.
947-1007, 947-8886
The Ward Warehouse, 521-6051
Kahala Mall, 732-1726
Sells surfboards, bodyboards, surf accessories, clothing

Waipahu Racquet Surf & Sports
1831 S. King St. #201, 941-4911
Sells surfboards, bodyboards, surf accessories

Xcel Hawaii
1116 Auahi St., 596-7441
New/used surfboards, surfing gear, wet suits, surf accessories

Waikiki

Boardriders Club
International Market Place, 926-5800
Kuhio Mall, 922-5900
Sells new surfboards, bodyboards, surf accessories, clothing

Hawaiian Island Creations
King's Alley, 971-6715
New, used, custom surfboards, bodyboards; surf accessories, clothing

Local Motion
1958 Kalakaua Ave., 979-7873
Sells & rents surfboards, bodyboards; surf accessories, clothing; repair service

Town & Country Surf Shop
Waikiki Trade Cntr., 923-9998
Hawaiian Regent Hotel
2552 Kalakaua Ave., 926-7954
Sells surfboards, bodyboards, surf accessories, clothing

Turbo Surf Design
1673 Kalakaua Ave., 946-1303
New, used, custom bodyboards; surf accessories

Waikiki Beach Services
Rents surfboards, bodyboards; surf instruction

Hawaii Kai

Local Motion
Koko Marina Shopping Cntr., 396-7873
Sells & rents surfboards, bodyboards; surf accessories, clothing; repair service

North Shore

Hawaii Surf & Sail
66-214 Kamehameha Hwy., 637-5373
Sells & rents surfboards, bodyboards, sailboards; surf accessories, clothing; repair service

Hawaiian Surf
North Shore Marketplace
66-250 Kamehameha Hwy., Haleiwa, 637-8316
New/used surfboards, surf gear/accessories

Ocean Sports with BK
66-215 Kamehameha Hwy., 637-4966
Sells surfboards, surf accessories, clothing; sells & rents bodyboards; repair service

Strong Current
North Shore Marketplace
66-250 Kamehameha Hwy., Haleiwa, 637-3406
Surf Museum, custom longboards, new longboards, classic used longboards, surf accessories, clothing

Surf & Sea, Inc.
62-595 Kamehameha Hwy., 637-9887
Sells & rents surfboards, bodyboards; surf accessories, clothing; repair service

Xcel Wetsuits Hawaii
66-4700 Kamehameha Hwy., 637-6239
Sells surfboards, bodyboards, surf accessories, clothing; repair service

Pearl City, Aiea

Hawaiian Island Creations
Pearlridge Shopping Cntr., 488-6700
Sells surfboards, bodyboards, surf accessories, clothing; repair service

Local Motion
Pearl Kai Cntr., 486-7873
Sells & rents surfboards, bodyboards, surf accessories, clothing; repair service

Town & Country Surf Shop
Pearlridge Shopping Cntr, 488-1055, 486-7378
Sells surfboards, bodyboards, surf accessories, clothing

Kailua, Kaneohe

Downing Hawaii
Windward Mall, 247-7400
New, used, custom surfboards, bodyboards; surf accessories, clothing

Hawaiian Island Creations
354 Hahani, Kailua, 266-6730
Sells surfboards, bodyboards, surf accessories, clothing; repair service

Kailua Sailboard Co.
130 Kailua Rd., 262-2555
Sells & rents sailboards, bodyboards;
surf accessories, clothing

Local Motion
Windward Mall, 263-7873
Sells & rents surfboards, bodyboards;
surf accessories, clothing; repair service

Maui

Hi-Tech
425 Koloa St., 877-2111
New, used surfboards, sailboards,
bodyboards; rents, repairs surfboards,
sailboards, bodyboards; surf acces-
sories, clothing

Honolua Surf Co.
845 Front St., Lahaina, 661-8848
Whalers Village, 661-5455
Lahaina Cannery Mall, 661-5777
2411 S. Kihei Rd., 874-0999
Surfboards, surf gear/accessories

Lightning Bolt Maui Inc.
55 Kaahumanu, Suite E, 877-3484
Sells & rents bodyboards, skateboards;
surf accessories, beachwear

Local Motion
Kihei: 1819 S. Kihei Rd., 879-7873
Lahaina: 1295 Front St., 661-7873
Sells & rents surfboards, bodyboards;
surf accessories, clothing; repair ser-
vice

Maui Tropics
90 Hana Hwy., 579-9816
1279 S. Kihei Rd., 875-8726
Sells surfboards, bodyboards, surf
accessories, clothing

Ole Surfboards
277 Wili Ko Place, 661-3459
Sells & rents surfboards; surf acces-
sories

Nancy Emerson's School of Surfing
244-SURF

Sailboards Maui Inc.
397 Dairy Rd., 871-7954
Sells & rents surfboards, bodyboards,
sailboards; surf accessories, clothing

Second Wind
111 Hana Hwy., 877-7467
Sells & rents surfboards, bodyboards,
sailboards; surf accessories, clothing

Windrigger Maui Ltd.
261 Dairy Rd., 871-7753
Sells & rents sailboards, surfboards,
bodyboards; surf accessories, clothing;
repair service, lessons

Kauai

Hanalei Surf Company
5-5161 Kuhio Hwy., 826-9000
Sells & rents surfboards, bodyboards,
sailboards; surf accessories, clothing,
lessons

Hawaiian Blades
3022 Peleke St., 245-9441
Custom surfboards

Kai Kane
Trader Building, Hanalei, 826-5594
Sells custom surfboards, surf acces-
sories, clothing; repair service

Kauai Water Ski & Surf Co.
4-356 Kuhio Hwy., 822-3574
Sells & rents surfboards, bodyboards,
wave skis, skimboards, kayaks; surf
accessories, clothing, repair service

Nukumoi
2100 Hoone Road, Poipu, 742-8019
New and used surfboards, bodyboards;
rentals of boards and beach gear; surf
accessories, clothing

Progressive Expressions
5428 Koloa Rd., 742-6041
Sells & rents surfboards, bodyboards;
surf accessories, clothing

Big Island

Big Island Cycle & Surf
Kamuela, 885-5005
Sells surfboards, bodyboards, wave
ski/skimboards; surf accessories, cloth-
ing, repair service

H20 Action Surf
Lanihau Cntr., 329-8962
New bodyboards, surf accessories,
clothing

Hobie Sports Kona
Kona Inn Shopping Village, 329-1001
Sells & rents surfboards, bodyboards;
surf accessories, clothing, repair ser-
vice

Local Style
Prince Kuhio Shopping Plaza #414
959-6121
Sells surfboards, bodyboards, skate-
boards, beachwear

Orchid Land Surfboards
262 Kamehameha Ave., 935-1533
Sells surfboards, bodyboards, surf
accessories, beachwear

CAMPING

OAHU

State Parks Division
Box 621, Honolulu, HI 96809
(808) 587-0300

STATE PARKS

Northeast Shore: Malaekahana Recreation Area, near Laie; Kahana Bay Beach Park, near Laie, Kanenelu

Southeast Shore: Waimanalo Bay Recreation Area, near Makapuu, Sandy Beach

South Shore: Sand Island Recreation Area, near Waikiki

City Dept. of Parks and Recreation
650 South King St.
Honolulu, HI 96813
(808) 523-4525

COUNTY PARKS

North Shore: Mokuleia Beach Park; Kaiaka Recreation Area, near Haleiwa

East Shore: Hauula Beach Park, Swanzy Beach Park, both near Laie, Kahuku

Southeast Shore: Bellows Field Beach Park, Waimanalo Beach Park, Makapuu Beach Park, all near Makapuu, Sandy Beach

West Shore: Kahe Point Beach Park, Nanakuli Beach Park, both near Tracks, Maili Point; Lualualei Beach Park, near Maili Point, Makaha; Keaau Beach Park, near Makaha, Yokohama

MAUI

Maui County Parks and Recreation
1580 Kaahumanu Ave.
Wailuku, Maui 96793
(808) 270-7389

State Parks Division
54 S. High St.
Wailuku, HI 96793
(808) 984-8109

STATE PARKS

East Shore: Waianapanapa, near Hana

KAUAI

Kauai County Parks and Recreation Dept.
444 Rice St. Room 230
Lihue, Kauai 96766
(808) 241-6670

COUNTY PARKS

North Shore: Haena Beach Park, Hanalei Beach Park, Anini Beach Park, all near Hanalei

East Shore: Hanamaulu Beach Park, Niumalu Beach Park, both near Lihue

South Shore: Salt Pond Beach Park, Lucy Wright Beach Park, both near Pakalas

State Parks Division
3060 Eiwa St.
Lihue, Kauai 96766
(808) 274-3444

STATE PARKS

West Shore: Polihale State Recreation Area

BIG ISLAND

Hawaii County Parks and Recreation
25 Aupuni St., Hilo, HI 96720
(808) 961-8311

COUNTY PARKS

Northeast Shore: Laupahoehoe Point Beach Park, near Waipio, Honolii; Kolokole Beach Park, Kealoha Beach Park, Onekahanaka Beach Park, all near Honolii; Isaac Hale Beach Park, near Kalapana

West Shore: Hookena Beach Park, Spencer Beach Park, both near Kailua-Kona

State Parks Division
Box 936
Hilo, HI 96721
(808) 974-6200 or (808) 329-6720

STATE PARKS

Northeast Shore: Kalopa Recreation Area, near Waipio

East Shore: MacKenzie Recreation Area, near Kalapana

Well, I'm battered and sore, but stoked to the core. I hope seeing my misadventures helps save you some pain and suffering. Later.